Praise for *Good God*

Not only is God not dead, but Lucas's book proves he is far better than we previously thought!

—Kevin Sorbo, actor, *God's Not Dead*

Lucas Miles has done it again! In *Good God* he writes about a God the world longs to know. His accurate understanding of God sheds the layers of religion and takes you to the core of knowing your Creator. After reading this book, you will feel enlightened, empowered, and privileged to know God.

—Tim Storey, pastor and celebrity life coach

Pastor Lucas Miles presents the grace of God in such a way that inspires and empowers others to step into their true identity in Christ. I am thankful for men of God like Lucas who present the transforming message of the gospel as *good* news!

—Cam McDaniel, University of Notre Dame running back

Lucas's dedication to his goals and dreams fuels his non-ending energy in pursuit of his destiny. I believe he will touch the world in a significant way.

—James B. Richards Ph.D., Th.D., author of *The Gospel of Peace* and *Grace: The Power to Change*

After years of stumbling through the shadows of religion, reading *Good God* is like finding a light switch in a dark room. Lucas Miles has guided us to freedom and truth in Christ after years of misunderstanding Christianity and the person of Jesus.

—Joanna Beasley, *American Idol* semifinalist and Christian recording artist

In my experience, the single greatest question people ask is, "How could a good God allow evil in the world?" In *Good God*, Lucas Miles not only answers the question but kicks in the door. This book is for anyone who has struggled with pain, disappointment, and tragedy, and it needs to be read by the most skeptical among us—which I have to admit, is far too often you and me.

—Phil Cooke, filmmaker, media consultant, and author of
One Big Thing: Discovering What You Were Born to Do

Lucas Miles is well qualified to write on the goodness of God. He has suffered loss and has heard the empty platitudes that often come with pain. In this book Lucas exposes the lunacy of blaming a good God for bad troubles. If you identify with Job or are troubled by hard times, *Good God* will help you walk in the freedom and healing of a good God who loves you like a Father.

—Paul Ellis, author of *The Hyper-Grace Gospel*

As he names some of life's most vexing issues, Lucas reminds us that one of the most difficult things to change is not just our hearts but our minds. This book not only opens up new ways of discovering ourselves but new ways of meeting God.

—Fr. Daniel G. Groody, C.S.C., University of Notre Dame

Lucas Miles's *Good God* will not just change the way you view God, but enable you to fall in love with a very good God who is a Lover desiring to be loved. It will give you a confidence to climb right up on the dear Father's lap! This book is a long overdue explanation of misunderstood and difficult passages, a revelation drawing us into the true heart of God.

—Jerry Grieser, author, *God's House of Mirrors*

The problem of evil in our current cultural context is a very real conversation piece. But there is something bigger: the view of God that we all hold. For far too long we have seen an old-man-up-there-somewhere trying to make sure we color in the lines only to crack us a good one if we miscue. Lucas wants to take that on idea, pick it apart, kick it aside, and show us how the texture and hue of life changes when the God who is good really comes to be known as the Good God. This is one you will want to read and then purchase a case to share with people who desperately want to believe in the message you find here!

—Dr. Ron Martoia, coach, consultant, and author of
Transformational Architecture and *Bible as Improv*

GOOD GOD

The One We Want to Believe In but Are Afraid to Embrace

LUCAS MILES

WORTHY®
PUBLISHING

Published by Worthy Books, an imprint of Worthy Publishing Group, a division of Worthy Media, Inc., One Franklin Park, 6100 Tower Circle, Suite 210, Franklin, TN 37067.

WORTHY is a registered trademark of Worthy Media, Inc.

HELPING PEOPLE EXPERIENCE THE HEART OF GOD

eBook available wherever digital books are sold.

Library of Congress Cataloging-in-Publication Data

Miles, Lucas, author.
 Good God : the one we want to believe in but are afraid to embrace / by Lucas Miles.
 pages cm
 ISBN 978-1-61795-672-0 (paperback)
 1. God (Christianity) 2. Christian life. I. Title.
 BT103.M55 2016
 231'.8--dc23
  2015032084

Unless otherwise noted, Scripture quotations are taken from The Holy Bible, New International Version®, NIV® Copyright © 1973, 1978, 1984, 2011 by Biblica, Inc.® Used by permission. All rights reserved worldwide. Scripture quotations marked NKJV are taken from the New King James Version®. Copyright © 1982 by Thomas Nelson. Used by permission. All rights reserved. Scriptures marked NASB are taken from the New American Standard Bible®, Copyright © 1960, 1962, 1963, 1968, 1971, 1972, 1973, 1975, 1977, 1995 by The Lockman Foundation. Used by permission. Scriptures marked MSG are taken from The Message. Copyright © 1993, 1994, 1995, 1996, 2000, 2001, 2002. Used by permission of NavPress Publishing Group. Scriptures marked KJV are taken from the King James Version of the Bible. Public domain.

Italics added to direct Scripture quotations are the author's emphasis.

Some names and identifying details have been changed to protect the privacy of the individuals involved.

For foreign and subsidiary rights, contact rights@worthypublishing.com

Published in association with Chaffee Management Group.

ISBN: 978-1-61795-672-0

Cover Design: Tobias' Outerwear for Books
Illustration: Clara Doti | MilesHerndon

Printed in the United States of America
16 17 18 19 20 VPI 8 7 6 5 4 3 2 1

To Krissy.

When I'm with you, I know God is good.

CONTENTS

GOD ISN'T RESPONSIBLE FOR YOUR PAIN

"WE NEED TO TALK," Jeff said, barging into my dorm room one night, almost pushing me over. I was a freshman at Purdue University, a Big Ten school, and my dorm floor, as you can imagine, was filled with all sorts of interesting characters—from computer nerds to frat boy hopefuls and everyone in between. A physics major, Jeff spent most days playing computer games, hacking websites, and writing code for friends. He was a tech zombie. On paper? A total geek. But as I would soon learn, there was more to Jeff than that—something deeper. He entered my room with such force that night that for a split second, I thought he was going to hit me.

"What's going on?" I asked, startled by the interruption. Jeff was obviously upset—almost violently so—and he looked as if he had been crying. He took a long, deep breath and then jumped right into it.

"When I was fifteen years old, I accidentally shot my sister with a hunting rifle. She died later that night. I heard you're a Christian. I want to know why God allowed my sister to die. We were just kids."

Having been open about my faith for as long as I can remember, I had gained a reputation as the "dorm-floor pastor," and this wasn't the first time someone had come to me with a question. Most of the time students asked me for relationship advice or intriguing philosophical questions initiated by midnight pizza runs and late nights spent at our favorite local café, both of which had a mystical way of drawing out questions about God. But that night was different. Jeff's question wasn't the typical coffee- or pizza-induced musing of a speculative college student. His question was real—a question originating not from the mind but from within the deep and painful recesses of his heart. And I knew, at that moment, I was completely ill equipped to answer it.

As I think back, I can't remember what I said to Jeff that night. As a college freshman, I'd had virtually no experience with personal tragedy. I had never even been to a funeral for anyone in my own family. I don't know what Jeff thought that night, but I'm certain that my muddled condolences didn't even come close to relieving the loss, hurt, and shame this young man carried around with him on a daily basis.

"WHY DID GOD ALLOW THIS TO HAPPEN?"

With time, I did become a pastor. As I ministered to people, I came to realize that Jeff's situation was not an isolated one. I encountered people who had experienced personal tragedy, lost loved ones, and been the victims of adverse circumstances. And I discovered that they all wrestled with the same question Jeff had:

"Why did God allow this to happen?"

The religious clichés I probably offered Jeff almost ten years prior were the same canned responses I was offering to the people I ministered to as a pastor, despite the fact that these responses offered little comfort. I knew God was good and that, somehow or other, all this pain couldn't be his fault. I just didn't know how to harmonize my belief in God's goodness with the tragedy I saw all around me and the scriptures that seemed to condone tragedy for the sake of our well-being. Despite what we learned in math class, when it comes to opinions about someone, the 10 percent bad always outweighs the 90 percent good and, for people facing tragedy, all of God's goodness witnessed in his creative work and the message of the cross fades as they entertain thoughts that he allows pain and heartache in their lives.

For several years, tragedy in my own life remained confined to philosophy term papers and theological speculations. But eventually I learned the hard way that tragedy always finds you—often when you least expect it. For our family it began during a routine physical for my wife, when she learned that her benign childhood heart murmur was the result of a bicuspid aortic valve in need of replacement. The news went from bad to worse as further tests revealed the weak valve was creating an irreversible aortic aneurysm that, if ruptured, would take her life. As a result, a highly invasive open-heart surgery was promptly scheduled.

In the days prior to her procedure, I remember making unnecessary late-night trips to the grocery store or driving aimlessly through the countryside only so I could leave the house to cry and scream at God, tearfully pleading with him to answer why he remained silent despite my wife's ever-deteriorating condition. Every day her aneurysm grew, and so did my questions and my doubts.

My only hope was to push through the assumptions I had about God and turn to Scripture in an attempt to see God for who he truly is. This began for me a period of intense study of what is often referred to as "the problem of evil." I devoured every section of Scripture I could find that dealt with topics such as suffering, discipline, the fall of man, the nature of God, trials and temptations, and the life of Christ. I tore through commentaries, word studies, and concordances hoping that, somewhere, I would find the answer I required.

I first turned to the book of Job, the cornerstone text for the church's current theology on suffering. I read and reread the book in more than a dozen Bible translations. With each new read, I sensed something was yet to be discovered within its text. God began revealing to me that asking God why is a question that doesn't merely challenge his decision-making but doubts his heart. In asking God why, I was assuming he was the source of the suffering and, ultimately, I was questioning his love for me. After much study, I found confirmation of God's goodness and love toward me in the Hebrew text of the book of Job.

> **Asking God why is a question that doesn't merely challenge his decision-making but doubts his heart.**

Unfortunately, for many people, the search for an answer to the problem of evil comes up empty, as any hope of a reply is muffled by the sounds of false teaching and anger against God. And the longer the question remains unanswered in our hearts, the stronger and more intense this anger grows within us.

As I came to learn, my issue (and, I believe, the issue of the entire world) is that we don't understand the true nature of God. It seems so elementary as I write it. Perhaps the simplicity of this truth has something to do with why it is so commonly overlooked. It just came down to this: I, like Job, didn't understand that God is good—*really good*—and I certainly didn't know how to communicate his goodness to others.

GOD ISN'T RESPONSIBLE FOR YOUR PAIN

One day my study of the problem of evil moved from mere academic ponderings to true revelation as I cried out in remorse for doubting God's intentions toward my wife and me. In that moment I had a profound realization: God was not the source of my pain, and my wife's heart problem wasn't God's will. That day, with tears in my eyes, I gained a heart knowledge regarding the goodness of God. I was free. For the first time, I shared the same eye-opening epiphany that Job uncovered after having his own heart-to-heart with God: "My ears had heard of you but now my eyes have seen you" (Job 42:5).

> God is neither responsible for your pain, nor is he allowing it. In fact, he is against it and wants nothing more than to prevent it.

As a result, today when I meet people like Jeff, my response is different. Without any doubt, I look them in the eyes and tell them, "God is neither responsible for your pain, nor is he allowing it. In fact, he is against it and wants nothing more than to prevent it." What you are about to read is the story of my journey into discovering the pure, unadulterated goodness of our God.

CHAPTER ONE

INVENTING GOD

The Answer Is in Our Hearts

SITTING SIDE BY SIDE on the decade-old sofa in my office across from my desk, Emily and Janelle couldn't have appeared more uncomfortable. Though in many ways opposites, neither of these high school students had been in a church building for quite some time. Emily was popular, pretty, had a bubbly personality, received good grades, and had a steady boyfriend. Janelle, on the other hand, was entrenched in Gothic subculture, seemingly trying to make herself less attractive with dark makeup; long, thick, unkempt hair; and a solemn stare that gave off an effective "don't look at me or talk to me" vibe. Despite her tremendous intelligence, Janelle was failing several of her classes.

These two girls were in court-ordered counseling as a consequence of smoking a joint outside of their high school a few weeks prior. Because of our church's reputation in the community, the judge felt that Oasis would be the place best equipped to try to reach them. As they sat silently pouting across from my desk, I couldn't help but wonder if their twelve weeks of court-ordered counseling sessions weren't also going to be equally as punishing for me.

"So let me get this straight," I said, breaking the silence. "You have to meet with me for twelve weeks in order to complete your probation?" *That's a long time,* I thought, *to talk with two students who show absolutely no interest in anything I might have to say.* "So what do *you* want to talk about for the next twelve weeks?" I asked in my best counselor voice. My question was predictably met with shrugged shoulders and blank stares. The remainder of our forty-five-minute session continued with more of the same. At this rate, it was going to be a long twelve weeks. As they exited, I knew I was going to have to get creative if I really wanted to help the two.

The next week, before the delinquent duo arrived, I set up a whiteboard with markers next to the couch. As they walked in, they took notice with curious glances.

"What's this for?" Emily asked.

"Today we're going to do something different," I responded. "Think of it like an experiment."

"Whatever," Janelle muttered. I obviously wasn't winning any popularity contests among my court-appointed pupils.

As they sat staring at the whiteboard, I began to explain to them that I had been thinking about their counseling and, instead of spending our sessions talking about the dangers of drug use as the court had suggested, I would rather talk about something more interesting—namely, "Who is God?" This caused Emily to giggle, appearing uncomfortable with the thought of talking about God for the remaining eleven weeks.

Janelle, much more bold with her disdain for the topic, proclaimed, "Just so you know, I don't believe in God."

"I thought you might say that," I responded. "So, for next week, I'd like for each of you to make a list of what you think God should be like if he *did* exist. I want you to describe a god you would want to believe in."

"You want us to make up a god?" Emily questioned.

"Exactly. I want you to invent a god you would believe in," I said.

As the session closed, I handed each girl a notebook and reminded them of their assignment. Little did I know how seriously both of them would take it.

When the following week rolled around, I couldn't help but be curious as to what this next counseling session would hold. Would they complete the assignment? Would any of this make sense to them? In a desire to help, I was banking on the truth found in Romans 1:19: "What may be known about God is plain to them, because God has made it plain to them." Before the session I said a quick prayer with this verse in mind and, just as I finished, I heard a knock at my door.

"Come on in," I welcomed them. "Did both of you bring your assignment?"

Both girls held up their notebooks. It was the first bit of enthusiasm I had seen in either of them since we began. As the session continued, I had the two of them write their lists on the whiteboard. Here is how they read:

If I could invent a god I would believe in, this is what he'd be like:
- My God would be *really* good.
- My God would always forgive me for messing up.
- My God would heal people who are sick.
- My God wouldn't be boring but fun.
- My God wouldn't allow bad things to happen.
- My God wouldn't send people to hell.
- My God would give his people superpowers to fight evil.
- My God wouldn't get mad at me if I failed, and he would always love me.
- My God would get rid of death so that people could live forever.

When the girls finished compiling their lists, which were almost identical, I asked them, "So, if God was like this, like everything on your list—you would believe in this God? You would give your life to follow him?"

They thought for a moment but seemed sufficiently confident that their god was far superior to my God—thus there was no danger of actually having to commit to follow this imaginary god. They both agreed: "Yeah, I would believe in a god like that."

From that session forward, the characteristics on the whiteboard were all we discussed in our counseling sessions. With each characteristic, I shared with the girls verses in the Bible that showed the god they thought they had invented was really the true God, the One and Only. My Romans 1:19 instinct was correct—what may be known about God was plain to them. I realized that their "invention" of God came so naturally because it was based in reality.

During our remaining counseling appointments, I learned that Janelle's hurt and distrust of God came from praying to him every night when she was ten as she watched her little sister die from a rare form of childhood cancer and that Emily's bubbly exterior was just a facade to hide the pain she felt from her parents' messy divorce. Like many, Emily and Janelle had misconceptions about God that led to their misgivings of him and their lack of desire to pursue him. As each session continued, the girls' hearts seemed to soften, and they started attending our church's youth ministry. A year later, Janelle, the self-proclaimed atheist, gave her life to Christ and was baptized.

I share this story with you to illustrate a point: in our hearts, we all carry an intuitive knowledge of who God is—his nature and his divine attributes. The problem is that most of us also carry with us a belief system about God, formulated through years of pain and religious indoctrination, that suppresses the truth of his goodness. All the while, the reality of who God really is remains sealed within our hearts.

In the case of Emily and Janelle, they knew in their hearts the true nature of who God is, but the pain of their past clouded their ability to embrace his actual identity, which in turn led to false conclusions about why certain tragedies happened in their lives, and what or who was the source of them. They, like most of us, responded in anger and rebellion toward God, which landed them on the couch in my office.

As we continued to meet together, however, I didn't have to convince them about God's good nature. I simply gave them the tools they needed to push past their pain in order to see God's genuine character. As Emily looked deeper, not only did she come to the conclusion that God had not caused her parents' divorce, but she was also able to remember numerous specific moments during that troubling time when God comforted and protected her. When Janelle discovered the truth of God that was written on her heart, she finally came to the conclusion that God did not allow her sister's tragic death. For both of them, the knowledge of God and his goodness was already present; I only helped remove the obstacles.

THE DAY THE WORLD CHANGED

There it was: an isolated tree standing near the center of the Garden. Not particularly handsome as far as trees go, but there was something alluring about it nonetheless. Its bark was gray and, despite being newly formed, it possessed a strange sense of age, old and hardened beyond its years. Its fruit, plump and lively, dangled from twisted branches and hung like ornaments shimmering in the sunset. Up until this day, the two of them had never noticed how enticing it appeared.

"So *this* is the tree he told you about?" the woman asked the man.

"Yes," he muttered, half embarrassed and half in awe of the mysterious tree. "Do you really think the serpent was right?" he inquired, somewhat hoping she would say no.

"Look at it! He has to be right. Have you ever seen a tree like this?" she said.

The two of them sat motionless, frozen by the weight of the moment, yet contemplating the decision they were about to make. The woman stepped confidently toward the tree and lunged forward on her tiptoes as far as she could to grab the ripest fruit she saw, plucking it from the branch. As she caressed the fruit between her delicate fingers, the man looked at her and said, "You know, after we do this . . . things won't be the same anymore."

"I know," she said excitedly. "The serpent said that once we eat it, we will be *like God*! Can you imagine?" She lifted the forbidden treasure to her lips and bit into the juicy, tender flesh. Then she playfully tossed it to her husband and he did the same. Words could not express the sweetness and flavor. But as delicious as that moment was, its savor quickly faded. Instantly they felt something new: *shame.* With one act of disobedience, the world as they had known it was changed. Their eyes were opened and they knew good. And they knew evil.

HUMANKIND: REFEREES OF MORALITY

From that fateful day, humanity and this world we call home were forever changed. When our first ancestors ate from that tree, humankind became fitted with an incredible intellect that enabled us to discern right or wrong, good or evil. This ability is a key differentiator between humans and the other created species.

In his classic book *Mere Christianity,* C. S. Lewis wrote this regarding our innate understanding of good and evil:

> This law was called the Law of Nature because people thought that every one knew it by nature and did not need to be taught it. They did not mean, of course, that you might not find an odd individual here and there who did not know it, just as you find a few people who are colour-blind or have no ear for a tune. But taking the race as a whole, they thought that the human idea of decent behaviour was obvious to every one. And I believe they were right.[1]

As we embark on our journey to discover this good God, we must solidify the fact in our minds that, as members of the human race, we have a unique ability to discern both good and evil. We can know and do know the difference. As our ancestors ate from that forbidden tree, their consciences—which prior to their disobedience had been pure, spiritual, and in tune with God's heart—instantly became cognizant of their own nakedness, their immorality. In the blink of an eye, Adam and Eve became keenly aware that they were no longer like God. Theologically speaking, they had gained knowledge of their own depravity. Sadly, this enlightenment was never meant to be. God never intended for mankind to tell the difference between us and him, and as a result, this one act plunged all of mankind into a never-ending cycle of questioning God's nature and his heart toward us, his beloved creation.

Before Adam and Eve gained this knowledge, ignorance of good and evil had prevented them from doubting God's love for them as they lived in blissful naiveté, enjoying unfettered relationship with God without the hindrances of guilt and shame. In their eyes and his, they were acceptable. Before the Fall, Adam and Eve knew they were God's beloved. Now, regardless of God's many attempts to communicate his love toward us, humans are driven by doubt and fear because we are keenly aware that our thoughts, desires, behavior, and nature fall incredibly short of God's goodness.

At the Fall humans became referees of our own morality, blowing the whistle on our fellow man and, at times, even shifting the blame onto God himself in our futile attempts to restore our righteousness and preserve our egos. "The woman *you* put here with me" and "The *serpent* deceived me" rang the sanctimonious excuses of Adam and Eve after the Fall (Genesis 3:12–13). As Eve pointed her finger at the serpent, Adam pointed to his wife for offering him the fruit and then to God for giving him the woman in the first place. Because of their awareness of their now fallen nature, Adam and Eve resorted to self-preservation at all costs—even if it meant blaming God. This was and is the nature of the curse and what causes us, even to this day, to cover ourselves in our own self-righteous fig leaves whenever we feel as if we are in danger of being exposed.

JUDGING GOOD FROM EVIL

In our frantic attempts at self-preservation, we have distorted the one unique skill we acquired at the Fall—the ability to judge good from evil. In order to sustain our dignity we have done the opposite of what our nature is inclined to do: we have resorted to calling what is good evil and what is evil good. As the events of our lives unfold, our interpretation of those happenings has caused us to invent a god who is the author of the beliefs we now have of ourselves.

For instance, some people refuse to accept their fallen state and futilely attempt to restore their perfect record by performing good deeds. Those who are guilt ridden embrace negative emotions, such as shame, as a self-imposed punishment for their wrongdoings. And the self-righteous refuse to accept any responsibility for their actions, always making excuses and blaming others for the substandard state of their lives. No matter the tendency, though, one thing is certain. As long as we perceive God as our enemy, we will continuously reinvent his nature in order to justify our circumstances.

Although Scripture clearly displays God's intentions for us to live an abundant life—the kind and quality of life that God himself has—many of us flounder, trapped in doubt, because we don't really know him. In John 10:10, Jesus clarified how we can discern the originator of circumstances in our lives: "The thief comes only to steal and kill and destroy; I have come that they may have life, and have it to the full." So there it is. In plain terms Jesus was saying, "If you are being stolen from, if your life is at stake, and if you are being destroyed—then Satan is responsible for that. But if you are experiencing the abundant life God intended, then

> **As long as we perceive God as our enemy, we will continuously reinvent his nature in order to justify our circumstances.**

that comes from me. I authored that." So why is it that when tragedy, theft, destruction, and death happen in our lives, we don't know whether to praise the God who gives and takes away or to resist the devil so that he will flee from us? Our theology has become our ball and chain. Our belief system has created our impotence.

But removing the obstacles that prevent us from embracing God's goodness can be challenging. I recently ran into a family friend at the supermarket. After he talked for several minutes about his son's impending death, he praised God for giving his unbelieving son a terminal illness, as he hoped it would finally set his son on a path to knowing Christ. He had been praying for God to use whatever means necessary in pursuit of his son's heart, and he perceived this illness to be God's effort at doing just that. As I quietly listened, my friend honored God for his so-called "goodness" toward his son. Yet I could see the sadness in his eyes at the thought of losing his son.

Even though my friend's heart was filled with negative emotion toward the situation, his theology was telling him to praise God for allowing it. While this man is perceived in the community to be a very godly man, it was clear that his understanding of God's nature had been blurred by his pain and religious indoctrination. His presumptions about God's character and workings were violating his innate knowledge of good and evil, yet he failed to let go of his beliefs. After all, his son's disease seemed to be an answer to his prayers.

I also once met with a young man held so captive by his fear of God that he wasn't sure if it was okay to shave his beard, because he didn't want to step out of God's will for his life. "But what if God doesn't want me to shave my beard?" he said. For him, the truth of God's goodness had been buried so deeply under years of religious teaching and expectations that he did not realize the god he was trying to measure up to wasn't really God at all. Rather, it was his own invention of God based upon his preconceived ideas about him. He was missing out on abundant life because of his fear of disappointing his idea of God; all the while, the true God was speaking to his heart, trying to get his attention.

DUE NORTH

So how do we get back on course, away from this invented god and back to the God of the Garden? We must embrace our inherent, internal compass of the difference between good and evil, which enables us to logically and systematically discern the cause and/or perpetrator of our circumstances. When we correctly identify the cause, we then know how to properly respond to the situation at hand.

For instance, if you wake up in the middle of the night to the sound of breaking glass, you must first determine the source of the commotion in order to respond appropriately. As you hear the sound and leap out of bed, you might grab a makeshift weapon such as a flashlight as you run to investigate the noise. What you uncover about the source of the broken glass, however, will determine your reaction. Maybe the wire holding up a picture frame has snapped, sending it crashing onto the hardwood floor below. Perhaps your youngest child stumbled and fell while trying to get a glass out of the cupboard, or maybe your rambunctious cat knocked over some dishes while running across the countertop. Your response to discovering your injured child would be quite different from your reaction to an intruder trying to enter through a window into your home. Although the noise sounds the same and both events result in broken glass on the floor, the cause is completely different and, therefore, so is your response. Our response must be appropriate to the cause.

Although we *should* apply this same logic to determining the real perpetrator of the events in our lives and the evil that is committed daily in our world, we inevitably fail to investigate our circumstances since we have been taught by religion that *everything* that happens is "God's will." We read in the Bible that God speaks to our hearts, but religious people tell us not to trust our instincts because God's ways are higher than our ways (Isaiah 55:8–9).

We will experience true freedom only when we shake off these religious clichés and legalistic pursuits and return to the proper understanding of God we had before the Fall. Fortunately for us, there is a new garden—what is referred to in Hebrews 4:10 as "God's rest"—a place that once we enter cannot be tainted by our misguided concepts of God. Only when we enter this garden are we able to find the good God we've been looking for.

BAIT AND SWITCH: JESUS AS TAUGHT BY THE CHURCH

As I travel the world, sharing with people about God's true nature, I've found that often the quickest way to end a conversation is by telling someone that I'm a pastor. I've sat beside fellow travelers on airplanes whose conversations with me take an immediate crash-landing after they ask me, "So what do you do?" As the words leave my mouth, many people's brains instantly filter terms like *pastor*, *church*, or *God* based upon their past experience with religion.

Those who have been hurt by religion tend to associate the pain of their past with the reminder of that pain in the present. If they were hurt or abused by religion or religious people in the past, then coming into contact with a pastor reminds them of their hurt. What they fail to realize is that they really aren't averse to God but rather to their *understanding* of God, which has become tainted and distorted through years of religious teaching, abuse, and pain.

A friend confided in me once that she was so scarred by her Christian upbringing that she was considering abandoning her religious heritage in pursuit of Eastern forms of spirituality. She had attended a Christian high school and concluded that the Jesus presented there was not sufficient for the needs of her heart.

If these experiences were isolated incidents, then perhaps they could be overlooked. But after more than fifteen years of ministry, I've found that the world is full of people with similar stories. The so-called "God" that religion proclaims is failing to reach the people who need him most. In Matthew 24:5, Jesus warned his disciples and, consequently, the church, saying, "For many will come in my name, claiming, 'I am the Messiah,' and will deceive many." This is exactly what has happened. While the church has been concerned about the rise of Islam and the claims of New Age thinkers, the enemy has presented to us a religious Jesus, a type of anti-Christ who appears in form and principle to be Jesus but whose character is vastly different.

POSTTRAUMATIC CHURCH DISORDER

A young woman in our ministry once labeled the hurts she had experienced at the hands of those in the church as "posttraumatic church disorder." How unfortunately appropriate! We can no longer ignore that the God the world has come to know through religion has long since deviated from the true God of the Bible. The real Jesus, who was and is God in the flesh, is alluring—not by his physical appearance but by his Spirit, who is filled with love and peace. During his ministry on earth, Jesus projected such magnetism that all who came across his path were drawn to respond to him in one way or another. Certainly religious people were offended when he walked this earth; but others, people like you and me, were filled with wonder. *Could this be the Messiah?* It was the question on everyone's mind. It was the hope that filled every heart.

While it's true that modern Christianity still rallies around "All you need is Jesus" and accepts a Christ-centered theology, both experientially and relationally our consciences are flooded with a list of New Testament rules and expectations that we're told we must follow in order to toe the line, maintain God's favor, and hang on to our own salvation.

John writes in chapter 8 of his gospel, "To the Jews who had believed him, Jesus said, 'If you hold to my teaching, you are really my disciples. Then you will know the truth, and the truth will set you free'" (vv. 31–32). We often mistakenly read Jesus' word "teaching" in this passage and invent a Jesus who is the deliverer of a new-and-improved list of obligatory rules from God. Using this idea of a new list of rules, some Christians have spiritually abused others by claiming people can come as they are to church but telling them later that they must shape up their lives in order to continue to be accepted by God and by others. In essence, we've traded Old Testament laws and regulations for New Testament principles and priorities. It's the same game—just under a different name.

But the word "teaching" in John 8:31 is singular. It's a subtle distinction, but with a dramatic difference. I believe Jesus was saying, "If you hold to *the* teaching"—as in the main teaching about him, who he is, and what he came to do—"then you are really my disciples and this truth will set you free." Jesus is urging us to permanently establish our hearts in the teaching of who he is—his nature. For you see, freedom comes from the teaching about Jesus and his goodness, not from merely keeping his commandments.

Hebrews 7:12 highlights that the real nature of the New Covenant looks *nothing* like the Old. "For when the priesthood is changed," the writer explains, "the law must be changed also." The writer continues in verses 18 and 19, "The former regulation is set aside because it was weak and useless (for the law made nothing perfect), and a better hope is introduced, by which we draw near to God." And then in verse 22, "Because of this oath, Jesus has become the guarantor of a better covenant."

I could write volumes on Hebrews 7 alone! In this chapter, the writer is revealing to us that now that Jesus has come, everything has changed. The old system, which was completely dependent upon us—our performance, our ability to keep the rules, and so forth—has been exchanged for the new system, which is based solely upon *Christ's* performance. As Hebrews 7:24–25 says, "But because Jesus lives forever, he has a permanent priesthood. Therefore he is able to save completely those who come to God through him, because he always lives to intercede for them." This precious salvation, which Jesus referred to in John 8, is now based upon Jesus' own performance—his priesthood, his eternal nature, his gift of righteousness, and his faithfulness. *This* is the teaching that now sets us free!

THE REAL JESUS

When Jesus walked the earth, something about him caused sinners and saints alike to gather around him everywhere he went. Has Jesus changed since then? Absolutely not! He is the same yesterday, today, and forever (Hebrews 13:8). What *has* changed is our understanding and communication of who Jesus is. The truth is that when Jesus walked on this earth, sinners ran to see him, touch him, and experience even a moment in his presence. Today, however, most people want nothing to do with the God religion has painted for this world. But I would venture to say that if the world were to see the *real* Jesus—this good God, the one who gained the attention of even the vilest of sinners— everyone would once again take note.

In Luke 18:18–19, Jesus encounters a man seeking clarification on how to inherit eternal life. Hoping to justify his own circumstances, the man addresses Jesus and says, "Good teacher, what must I do to inherit eternal life?" Jesus responds by asking, "Why do you call me good? No one is good—except God alone." Jesus is forcing this man to make a choice; he is drawing out the truth of the man's heart. He is stating, "You can call me teacher, but don't call me good, unless you believe that I am, in fact, God—because only God is good."

This is the question we all must answer in our own hearts. Do we really believe that the Jesus we call upon is *good*? Because until we are truly convinced that he is good, we cannot be convinced that he is God. Perhaps that seems elementary to some. But I want to challenge you to consider this: Is the God you believe in actually good?

INVENTING GOD IN OUR HEARTS

As Proverbs 4:23 informs us, the heart is the source of all issues of life. All our beliefs flow from our hearts, including our beliefs about God. In this way, our hearts, too often guided by pain and self-preservation, shape our beliefs and opinions of God. As George Bernard Shaw is credited with saying: "God created us in his image, and we decided to return the favor." So we fabricate a god to fit our needs and justify our circumstances. Essentially, we have invented a god to match the level of our understanding and to comfort our pain.

> **Is the God you believe in actually good?**

As a result, the god we are left with is hardly a good God at all. This ultimately affects our fellowship with the real God. Colossians 1:21 explains it this way: "Once you were alienated from God and were enemies in your minds because of your evil behavior." God was never against us per se, but because we viewed God a certain way (as judgmental, angry, and incapable of loving people like us), we distanced ourselves from him and failed to receive his grace. The Israelites reacted the same way when God met with Moses on Mount Sinai. Originally, God's intent was to meet with *all* of the people (Exodus 19:10–11). Yet despite God's intention to fellowship with the people, we learn that God's desires were not fulfilled. Because of the Israelites' fear of God, the people remained at a distance (Deuteronomy 5:4–5).

Today, we, too, are in danger of misjudging God and following the example of the Israelites by staying at a distance. Yet to do so would be to miss out on the life, joy, and power of knowing our Savior, Jesus Christ—who is God in the flesh. For this reason, we must unpack our misguided concepts of God and begin to see him as he truly is.

CHAPTER TWO

GOD IS NOT A CRIMINAL

God Didn't Do It

LET'S FACE IT: God has a bad reputation. If a child dies, we say God took him because he needed another angel in heaven. If a hurricane strikes, we say God sent it because of the sinfulness of the region. If a woman loses her job or becomes stricken with cancer, we say God is trying to get her attention.

But the blame doesn't stop there. God has even become the scapegoat for what people say he does not directly do. How many times have you or others spoken these words: "God might not have caused it, but he allowed it"? You see, religion has painted a picture of God as one who has the power to stop a crime but, for reasons too high for us to understand, allows tragedies in our lives in order to teach us a lesson.

One might assume that such accusations against God could be propagated only by a slanderous enemy, but, amazingly, we Christians are all too often the ones perpetuating this spiritual nonsense. If you don't believe me, then try to stick up for God and clear his name in conversations regarding personal or global tragedy. My guess is you will likely be bombarded with arguments about suffering and free will, quotes from the book of Job, and personal testimonies of how God caused suffering in a person's life in order to bring that person closer to him. What's even more shocking is that those who hold on to such beliefs don't intend them to be insults toward God, or even accusations against him. Rather, Christians intend these statements to be praise for their mighty Creator! For in our hearts, we cannot accept a God who is truly good in the face of the tragedies and hardships that exist in the world he created.

Everyone can comprehend an evildoer who gets what he has coming to him. We're comfortable with that. In fact, when it happens in the movies, we cheer for it. But when the innocent undergo senseless tragedy, their suffering is beyond our ability to comprehend.

Naturally, our reaction to crises and problems is to try to make sense of them. Looking for understanding and relief, we embrace a theology that says everything happens for a reason and hold to the hope that God must have somehow intended this tragedy for our good. After all, doesn't Romans 8:28 tell us that "in all things God works for the good of those who love him, who have been called according to his purpose"? Yes! But God's working things together for our good doesn't presuppose that he authored the tragedy in the first place. Simply put, saying that God brings good out of bad circumstances does not imply that he allowed the negative circumstances to happen in the first place. We must begin to see our tragedies for what they really are, instead of spiritualizing our circumstances in order to find purpose in our hardships and to help us cope with the sufferings of this life.

Unfortunately, this theology is taught in sermons every Sunday in churches across the world where this sort of thinking is commonplace. Although accepting a "God allowed it" theology brings initial relief, if left unchallenged it creates distrust toward God. If we see God as the one *causing* or even *allowing* our pain, then we will be paralyzed from standing our ground against the real perpetrator, the devil.

After all, if God is the culprit behind humankind's suffering, then who could stand against him or his will? If we embrace this lie, then we will continue to feel alienated from the one who can offer the real solution to our problem. The truth is that God is not the source of our pain. In fact, if you believe that God is causing your problems, or even allowing these problems in the traditional sense of the word, then you've already abandoned the God of the Bible before your journey to uncover his goodness has even begun.

GOD ON TRIAL

A few years ago, national news agencies reported about a young man who was arrested due to his involvement in a double homicide case. It was a brutal incident, where gang members used information the young man gave them to break in to a house and burglarize it. Although no one was supposed to be home at the time of the crime, the burglars were interrupted by two gardeners who were tending the lawn in the backyard. Upon being discovered, the gang members gruesomely murdered the gardeners. While the young man did not shoot anyone himself, nor was he even present at the time of the murders, he was still convicted of felony murder. He was sentenced to 125 years in prison due to his involvement in allowing the crime to take place by providing information about the family's home and by refusing to notify the authorities of the impending robbery. Responding to the young man's sentence, a family member of one victim commented that without the young man, her husband would still be alive.

You see, even in our modern court system we recognize that being associated with a crime demands the same level of justice as being the perpetrator of the crime. Consider what Martin Luther King Jr. once said: "He who passively accepts evil is as much involved in it as he who helps to perpetrate it. He who accepts evil without protesting against it is really cooperating with it."[1] In our society we call out our Christian brothers and sisters for passively allowing hate and injustice to occur, yet we praise God for doing the same thing! It just doesn't make sense. For God to cause evil, or even to allow or accept evil, would cease to make him good and, thus, cease to make him God. Yet many religious people, full of good intentions, cling to this doctrine, not realizing that what they are holding on to is spiritually killing them.

Recently I watched a national news show interview a pastor about tornadoes that had devastated his region. The pastor said, "You really don't know what you're made of until God puts you through a test like this." If that were an isolated belief, then it would be easy to overlook, but it's not. Similar sentiments were uttered by church leaders and pastors about such incidents as Hurricane Katrina, 9/11, and the Oklahoma City bombing. Some view these and other happenings as God's judgment against our nation. Others profess ignorance as to why God "allowed" a particular tragedy, simply saying, "God's ways are higher than our ways" and claiming the tragedy was ultimately "for God's glory." If this were true, then we should abandon the pursuit of America's most wanted, because God seems to be the real villain.

> For God to cause evil, or even to allow or accept evil, would cease to make him good and, thus, cease to make him God.

Think about these accusations for a second. Do these actions really seem like the workings of Jesus? The God who became flesh and gave his life for the sins of the entire world? Traditional Christian theology, whether we like it or not, has made God out to be a criminal. We've not only misunderstood him, but we've also slandered his character and falsely accused him. The above claims aren't the actions of a good God but of a sadistic, egotistical maniac. Jesus is not a terrorist. He doesn't blow up buildings for his glory. And he won't give you sickness, like some sort of biological warfare, in order to get you to turn to him for the antidote. Additionally, God is not just sitting back *allowing* evils like this to happen, as though he were a terrorist sympathizer or lazy superhero.

The problem with most "God allowed it" doctrines is that we don't take them to the extreme. Sure, it sounds spiritual to say that God allowed something to happen. But place him in the room while it's happening. Would a good God just sit back in a room and watch a young girl getting molested or raped, and do nothing about it? Would you? I know I wouldn't. So are we somehow better than God?

Some might be thinking, *But God watched his own Son die a horrific, torturous death and didn't stop it. So why wouldn't he treat me—his son by faith—the same way?* Let us not forget that Jesus is God! God gave up his *own* life through Christ the Son. He did this so that we could reign with him (Romans 5:17). In fact, the Bible teaches that the Lamb "was slain from the creation of the world" (Revelation 13:8). God—Father, Son, and Holy Spirit—was in agreement from the foundation of the world to offer the Son (i.e., the Lamb) as a sacrifice and substitute for the sins of his children.

Why would God ever want us to experience the very thing he died to free us from?

GOD: BOTH GOOD AND ABLE?

I think that most of us want to believe that God is good, but we cannot find a way to harmonize God's goodness with the evil that exists in this world. In an attempt to do so, one might ask, "Are you saying God isn't able to stop the evil in this world? This is why bad things happen?"

These questions reveal something about our thoughts regarding the nature of God. We are more comfortable sacrificing some of God's goodness than altering his power. That is, we would rather believe in a God who is all-powerful than believe in a God who is all-good. We reason, *Either God has the power to do something about evil but chooses to allow it for reasons we cannot understand, or he has no power to stop the evil, which makes him no god at all.*

David Hume wrote about this dilemma in his work *Dialogues Concerning Natural Religion*. In it he quotes Epicurus, a Greek philosopher: "Is he willing to prevent evil, but not able? Then is he impotent. Is he able, but not willing? Then is he malevolent. Is he both able and willing? Whence then is evil?"[2] Like Hume, in our minds "God is good" *or* "God is able" are the only two options. Thankfully, as we'll see later, the Scriptures hold the truth about God, which sacrifices neither his goodness *nor* his power.

THE TRINITY IS NOT A MULTIPLE PERSONALITY DISORDER

In the 1932 World Series at Wrigley Field in Chicago, Babe Ruth of the New York Yankees, with two strikes against him, stepped away from the plate and, in a now-famous prophetic gesture, held up his bat and pointed to the center-field wall. Then, as the next pitch came, the Babe swung and heroically connected with the curve ball, sending it soaring over center field for a home run, as he had predicted. Though there is some dispute as to whether he was actually pointing to the pitcher or to the center-field wall, the story stuck and has since become fixed in baseball history.

In the same way, two thousand years ago, the great Jesus Christ, at the start of his ministry, walked into a Nazarene synagogue, picked up the scroll of Isaiah, and read this: "The Spirit of the Lord is on me, because he has anointed me to proclaim good news to the poor. He has sent me to proclaim freedom for the prisoners and recovery of sight for the blind, to set the oppressed free, to proclaim the year of the Lord's favor" (Luke 4:18–19). Long before Babe Ruth's historic gesture, Jesus held up the prophet's scroll and read this passage with an expectant confidence, announcing his mission on earth. At that moment, he was declaring, "Regardless of what symbolic pitches the devil throws—whether poverty, sickness, oppression, or anything else—I will redeem them all."

For some reason, divine benevolence is easy for us to accept about Christ but difficult for us to embrace about God.

Instead of God being three in one, we've made him out to have a multiple personality disorder, segregating his characteristics into specific parts of the Trinity. God carries with him wrath, justice, and holiness. Christ is the bearer of love, grace, and mercy. And the Holy Spirit? Well, he is the unpredictable, strange, and mysterious wind who blows in like the weird uncle at your family reunions. A God this confused needs to be committed.

Have we forgotten that each person of the Godhead is one and the same, coexisting in equality? Hebrews 1:3 states without question that Jesus "is the radiance of God's glory and the exact representation of his being, sustaining all things by his powerful word." This means if we want to know what God is like, all we have to do is look at Jesus, for he is the complete and perfect reflection of God! Each member of the Godhead possesses the same nature, attitude, characteristics, purpose, and will. The members of the Trinity are indistinguishable from one another, for they are one and the same. As Jesus is, so is the Father and so is the Spirit.

THE DANGER OF EITHER/OR THINKING

The disconnect in this either/or thinking is that we often approach the study of the nature of God by looking at the Old Covenant instead of starting with the person of Christ. Hebrews 10:1 tells us, "The law is only a shadow of the good things that are coming." The law is a shadow designed to point to Jesus—God's goodness incarnate. But if we look only at the shadow of

God, revealed to us through the Old Covenant, then we will remain unable to distinguish God's complete features, which are only seen in the person of Christ.

To illustrate this further, if your two-year-old son and his ten-year-old brother stood in a doorway, and you could only see their shadows being cast into the room, you could still distinguish the boys from one another. In fact, if you saw just one of their shadows, you could understandably begin a conversation with either of them, already determining their identity before they fully came into your line of sight. For if you intimately know a person, then his shadow is easy to recognize. But if you are unfamiliar with a person's true identity, then a shadow is not enough evidence to produce a clear perspective. This is why we must start our pursuit to discover the true heart of God by looking at the person of Jesus Christ, rather than at the shadow his glory cast in the Old Covenant.

Because religious people too often focus on the Old Covenant God, religion has painted a picture of him as a God who allows and even gives diseases, only for his alter ego Jesus to heal; a God who puts you down, only later to lift you up; a God who saves you from your sins, only to have the Holy Spirit convict you of your faults. This type of behavior is like a magician who resorts to planting people in the crowd to show off his greatness. Or like an underappreciated police officer who places a bomb, only later to "discover" it, disarm it, and get his picture on the front page of the paper along with a medal from the mayor. Thankfully God doesn't work like this.

THE DILEMMA

At one time, I was afraid that by embracing God's goodness, I would somehow lose sight of his wrath and justice. Others I've spoken to are fearful of believing the wrong thing or of making some sort of theological blunder that would disqualify them for their secure place in glory. I believe we all have obstacles or limiting beliefs we allow to paralyze us in our pursuit to discover God's goodness.

Take Alex, for instance. I met Alex at a local coffee shop. He was a friendly yet somewhat socially awkward man in his early forties. He approached me while I was reading my Bible one morning, asked to sit with me, and began asking me about what I believed. We both were regulars at this particular café, so this first meeting turned into a dozen or more talks about faith and theology.

> **We all have obstacles or limiting beliefs we allow to paralyze us in our pursuit to discover God's goodness.**

As I got to know Alex better, I learned that he had been the victim of decades of brutally strict legalistic teaching. He had been taught that faith plus obedience equals salvation, and as a result, he lived in constant fear for his eternal fate. During one of our coffee conversations, while discussing spiritual identity, he said it finally clicked. For the first time in his life, he realized who he was in Christ. The next week he showed up at our church, but later he told me he couldn't convince himself to get out of his car and walk into our building. He had grown up in a denomination that forbade musical instruments during worship, and because he could hear the worship band rehearsing before the service started, he became paralyzed with fear. He wanted to believe in the goodness of God but, because of his fear of making a mistake or offending God, he allowed a set of drums and a couple of guitars to prevent him from experiencing God's goodness that day. He told me he had wanted so badly to come into the service, but he was just too afraid.

This dilemma isn't new. Jonah couldn't get past God's mercy for the people of Nineveh. In Jonah 1:2, God tells Jonah, "Go to the great city of Nineveh and preach against it, because its wickedness has come up before me." As a good prophet, you would expect that Jonah would be on the first ship to Nineveh, but he wasn't. Instead, we find him on a ship heading the *opposite* direction. Why? Jonah reveals the reason for his unwillingness to go to Nineveh in Jonah 4:2–3: *"I knew that you are a gracious and compassionate God, slow to anger and abounding in love, a God who relents from sending calamity.* Now, Lord, take away my life, for it is better for me to die than to live." Like so many, Jonah was offended by God's goodness. He would rather die than see the wretched people of Nineveh become recipients of God's grace. Sure, he was obedient in eventually going to Nineveh—but, in the end, Jonah pouted indignantly that God had spared the longtime enemies of Israel.

Jonah isn't alone in choosing zeal over love. The Pharisees, too, were afraid of the consequences of setting aside God's law to approve of Jesus healing on the Sabbath (Luke 13:10–17). Their zealousness for the Mosaic Law completely overshadowed their willingness to see people set free, which resulted in an inability to embrace the gifts and blessings of God.

GOD'S LOVE IS HIGHER THAN OUR LOVE

Somewhere in our journey to discover God, we, like Jonah, have become offended by God's goodness. And like a young child filling a jar with fireflies, we've attempted to catch God's goodness, quantify it, and put limitations on it, making sure not to let it escape our grasp. But God's love has no rules or bounds. "Exactly," some will say. "You can't confine God to looking a certain way or always doing a certain thing. Sometimes God allowing tragedy in a person's life might *be* the highest form of love for them. After all, aren't God's ways higher than our ways?"

This perspective is quite common, and perhaps some of you reading this have thought the same thing. In order to clarify what exactly are God's ways, let's read the first nine verses of Isaiah 55, in which this thought can be found.

"Come, all you who are thirsty,
　　come to the waters;
and you who have no money,
　　come, buy and eat!
Come, buy wine and milk
　　without money and without cost.
Why spend money on what is not bread,
　　and your labor on what does not satisfy?
 Listen, listen to me, and eat what is good,
　　and you will delight in the richest of fare.
Give ear and come to me;
　　listen, that you may live.
I will make an everlasting covenant with you,
　　my faithful love promised to David.
See, I have made him a witness to the peoples,
　　a ruler and commander of the peoples.
Surely you will summon nations you know not,
　　and nations you do not know will come running to
　　you,
because of the LORD your God,
　　the Holy One of Israel,
　　for he has endowed you with splendor."

Seek the LORD while he may be found;
    call on him while he is near.
Let the wicked forsake their ways
    and the unrighteous their thoughts.
Let them turn to the LORD, and he will have mercy on
    them,
    and to our God, for he will freely pardon.

"For my thoughts are not your thoughts,
    neither are your ways my ways," declares the LORD.
"As the heavens are higher than the earth,
    so are my ways higher than your ways
    and my thoughts than your thoughts."

As you read these verses, did you note that nowhere in the context of this passage are God's higher ways described as tragedy and hardship? In fact, let's consider the higher ways and higher thoughts of God listed in Isaiah 55.

Through the prophet Isaiah, God is imploring us to come and be refreshed, regardless of our ability to pay for it. God further promises to give us water, food, wine, and the richest of fare. He speaks of his covenant with humankind and his faithful love that extends to the people because of his promise to his servant David. Then, perhaps most noteworthy, the prophet continues by informing us that even wicked and evil people can turn to the Lord and find mercy and be pardoned of their sins (v. 7). After considering all of this, we read in verses 8 and 9: "For my thoughts are not your thoughts, neither are your ways my ways." No mention of tragedy. No talk of hardships. No discussion of car accidents, heart attacks, or cancer. God simply offers his grace, even to those who do not deserve it.

When we read this passage in context, we see that God's higher ways are his love, which is higher than our love; and his mercy, which is higher than our form of mercy. We sell our goods for a price, but God gives "without cost" the "richest of fare" to those who have need. We fail at keeping our commitments, but God is faithful to his covenants. We heap judgment and condemnation on the wicked, but God freely pardons those who put faith in him. Our love is limited, but God's love has no bounds and his goodness fills the heavens. In all of these aspects, God's ways are higher than our ways.

GOD IS GOOD—THE DEVIL IS BAD

We read earlier in John 10:10 that Jesus says, "The thief comes only to steal and kill and destroy; I have come that they may have life, and have it to the full." The question remains: "Do we really believe God?" Do we believe that Jesus came to give us life? Do we believe that God's intentions toward us are good and that it is Satan who is the author of the evil in this world?

Many of us try to sidestep these questions by focusing our attention on controversial passages of Scripture, as well as on our own experiences, instead of embracing the simplicity of the gospel. My point isn't that we shouldn't concern ourselves with unpacking difficult passages—in fact, I've devoted the majority of this book to dealing with such issues; rather, we must first look to the person of Jesus, God in the flesh, and determine whether we really believe him to be good.

It cannot be both ways. God is either completely good or something altogether inferior. When it comes down to it, biblical theology is simple. God is good and the devil is bad. God wants to give us life; the devil wants to take it. The problem is that, for many of us, our belief system diminishes God's goodness and fails to take seriously the malevolence of the devil. To move forward, we must consider them both.

CHAPTER THREE

SOVEREIGN GOD OR CONTROL FREAK?

God Is Not a Baby Snatcher

IT WAS THE WEEK the world stopped. At least at our house.

After years of doctors' appointments monitoring my wife's congenital heart defect, and her subsequent eighteen-month recovery after her open-heart surgery, we were more than ready to start a family. We tried for more than two years after her valve replacement before we finally received the incredible news that we were expecting.

Like many couples, we waited as long as we could before announcing our pregnancy. When we finally broke the news, my wife was ten and a half weeks pregnant and we decided to make the announcement from the stage on a Sunday morning at our church. So after I finished preaching, I called Krissy onstage and together we announced to the congregation that we were having a baby. The news was received with cheers and enthusiastic applause. It was a beautiful day. We were parents.

That next Friday, while having lunch with a friend, I received a call from my wife. When I answered the phone, she barely said a word. She just sobbed. And I knew. Throwing some cash down on the table, I ran out the door. Luckily, I was close by and raced home to take her to the hospital, but it was too late. Our baby—little Charlotte Grace Miles—had miscarried and gone home to be with Jesus.

Like many after experiencing such loss, that week was filled with deep sorrow and an unexpected pain we had never experienced before. To be frank, it was hellish. We didn't eat, we barely slept, and I don't think either of us left the house for almost a week.

During that time, our house was flooded with compassionate friends, family, and church members who showered us with fruit baskets, meals, and flowers. Some prayed for us, others simply left items at the door, and perhaps my favorites were those who just hugged us tightly without saying a word.

One dear friend came by to offer her support. "You know why this happened, don't you?" she said with a caring twinkle in her eye. We braced ourselves, like the scene in the movie you know is coming but you don't want to open your eyes to see it. She continued, "Your little girl was so loved by God that he couldn't stand to be apart from her for one second," she offered with what I'm sure was the kindest of intentions.

After suffering the biggest loss of our lives, my wife and I were expected to be comforted by the thought that God took our baby. Not that the miscarriage happened by accident or because there was perhaps a problem with the fetus, but God did it—really? He took our baby so that she could be with him instead of us? He gave her to us, but then he decided after a few short weeks that she was more important to him than we were, so he took her and left us with nothing?

To be honest, Krissy and I knew it was only a matter of time before someone responded to our loss like this, and we were more dumbfounded than surprised. Fortunately, our understanding of God's true nature had been well established long before this happened, and while the woman's response to our loss was much like the condolences countless people regularly receive after tragedy strikes, my wife and I knew better than to believe that God was responsible.

I wish everyone were so convinced.

THE SOVEREIGNTY OF GOD

"Jesus rules the wind. The tornadoes were his," said one well-known pastor in response to a deadly string of over ninety tornadoes that demolished towns in approximately a dozen states and killed forty-one people in 2012. He said, "We do not ascribe such independent power to Mother Nature or to the devil. God alone has the last say in where and how the wind blows. If a tornado twists at 175 miles an hour and stays on the ground like a massive lawnmower for 50 miles, then God gave the command."[1]

If I read this quote at any Bible college or at any given church around the United States, hardly anyone would blink an eye. Why? Because the thought that God is in control of all the happenings of this world has become so pervasive that it has become a cornerstone of Christian doctrine and theology. No one even questions it anymore.

If you don't believe me, just tune in to your local Christian radio station. Many popular Christian worship songs describe heartache and pain and then attribute them to God's work in their lives. Or turn on a Christian television channel, where you will hear sermons by popular Christian pastors who teach that nothing is out of the control or reach of God's sovereignty.

Though the Bible never mentions these terms, Christian theology insists that God is all-present, all-knowing, and all-powerful. In the Western world, we coined the terms *omnipresent*, *omniscient*, and *omnipotent*, then lumped them together to form the popular "extreme sovereignty of God" doctrine. I like to add the adjective *extreme*, due to the three prevailing thoughts behind this concept:

1. God is in control.
2. God either causes or allows everything.
3. Everything happens for a reason.

In this *extreme* sovereignty doctrine, all events in this life must pass across God's supernatural presidential desk of the universe, while all of creation waits to see what he chooses to approve or veto. Once the verdict is in, God's methods have no restrictions, his intentions remain unknown, and his will remains a mystery. The extreme sovereignty of God doctrine is the most harmful message that has evolved out of the church in recent history.

The Common Christian View of Sovereignty

John Calvin, a Protestant Reformer responsible for shaping much of today's Christian theology, said this:

> There is always the best reason, no doubt, for every thing that God does; but he often conceals it from us for a time, in order to instruct us not to be wise in ourselves, but to depend entirely on the expression of his will. . . . When Christ permitted his disciples to be tossed about in a perilous condition, for a time, by an opposing storm, it was to fix their attention more powerfully on the assistance which he brought to them.[2]

Calvin's God, it seems, is willing to create life-threatening circumstances to elicit fear, which is then used to gain our trust. Calvin's God sends storms and allows his people to face near death in order to teach them obedience. Like the underappreciated police officer mentioned in the last chapter, Calvin's God secretly plants hardship in order to appear the hero once his people are rescued from harm's way.

Although the idea that God is in control has become a normal way of viewing God, it sadly leaves people to assume that everything that happens in their world was either approved by or caused by our heavenly Father. And for those going through untold heartache, this is not only a tough message to swallow, but sends a mixed message about God's boundless love and grace.

SOVEREIGNTY IN SCRIPTURE

Some might be surprised to discover that the word *sovereign* never appears in the King James Version of the Bible. While it is found over three hundred times in the Old Testament of the New International Version of the Bible—as in "sovereign God"—it is simply used as a moniker equivalent to what is translated in the King James Version as "Lord God." In fact, never in one instance, even in the New International Version, is "sovereign" used to describe God in the sense of "controlling everything."[3] And although God is commonly described in our Christian culture this way through our depiction of him as omniscient, omnipresent, and omnipotent, these God-identifiers are also never found in Scripture.

To a Hebrew, God was understood through the lens of his *redemptive* characteristics, which depicted his role in their lives and his good nature toward them. This is exactly why the Hebrews referenced him repeatedly not just as God but as "God Our Peace," "God Our Shepherd," "God Our Healing," "God Our Righteousness," "God Our Sanctification," "God Our Provision," and so on. Ironically, in all these names, understood by the Israelites from generations past, God was never referred to as being "in control" or "sovereign" the way we think of these terms today.[4] The misunderstanding stems from a poor translation of the Hebrew name for God, *Adonai*, which, according to Hebrew lexicons, means "my lord" and carries with it no additional commentary on God's actions or nature. There is no way around it; the religious notion of sovereignty is not in the original text—it has been added.

With the influence of Western thinking, a historical and cultural shift occurred from understanding God in terms of his *good nature* to primarily viewing him in light of his all-encompassing *power*. Yet in days of old, as we saw in the afore-mentioned examples, the focus of God's name was never placed on his power itself but on the *purpose* of his power. For example, his power was available to redeem, to provide, to sanctify, to heal, to bring peace, to offer righteousness, and so forth. God's redemptive names, therefore, from a Hebrew understanding, became the outline of his nature and provided the blueprint and reference point for his goodness.

I actually agree that God is, in fact, sovereign. Yet I do not think he is sovereign in the way religion has come to define *sovereignty*. If we set aside the religious notion of *sovereign* for a moment and simply look at the dictionary definition, we see that *sovereign* means "having supreme rank, power, or author-ity."[5] So, semantically speaking, yes, God *is* sovereign. He has supreme rank. He holds supreme power and he operates in supreme authority. Yet in not one of those definitions could God be referenced as "controlling everything."

GOD IS SOVEREIGN OVER HIMSELF

In the "two-by-four talks" of 1989, the two Germanys and the four World War II Allies officially declared Germany to be a free nation, and as such, the Allies granted Germany "complete and unrestricted sovereignty." What did that mean exactly? It meant that after decades of occupation and oppression by other countries, Germany was granted the authority to govern itself freely according to its own rules and established rights and privileges.

In the same way, the United States is also considered a sovereign nation. We are free to govern ourselves. Right or wrong, we elect our own officials, write our own laws, and uphold our own policies. But even with all of our power as a nation, we don't run the world, nor are we able to dictate the affairs of nations that reject our influence or opinion. The fact that North Korea and Iran still have nuclear programs is proof of this. The United States is sovereign, but only in relation to itself.

Consequently, for God to be a god who is all-knowing, all-present, and all-powerful, he must also therefore maintain the ability to rule himself and freely choose how to dictate his own power, knowledge, and presence. God's greatest feat of strength is being able to govern his own ability, displaying that his attributes are neither greater nor more all-encompassing than he himself is. God alone is the one who controls and defines his attributes; his attributes cannot be defined by us.

As a result, it's important to understand that God has no limits except those that he places on himself. Most people would be surprised to know that the Bible is full of actions that God either couldn't or wouldn't do! Furthermore, whatever God speaks, he can *never* rescind, for he cannot nullify what he promises. For him to do so would be for him to violate his own words and compromise his faithfulness—something God promised he would never do!

Here are just a few examples of things God cannot do:

- God cannot disown himself (2 Timothy 2:13).
- God cannot lie (Numbers 23:19; Hebrews 6:18).
- God cannot be tempted by evil (James 1:13).
- God cannot remember your sins (Hebrews 8:12).
- God cannot tempt anyone (James 1:13).
- God cannot change (James 1:17).
- God cannot take back his word (Psalm 89:34).

In addition to the above mentioned things that God cannot do, the Bible even says that God, at times, even limits what he knows. For example, in Jeremiah 19:5, the Bible states that the vile activities of the Israelites *never* even entered into the "all-knowing" mind of God! Consider also perhaps one of the saddest scriptures in the Bible:

> The LORD saw how great the wickedness of the human race had become on the earth, and that every inclination of the thoughts of the human heart was only evil all the time. *The LORD regretted* that he had made human beings on the earth, and his heart was deeply troubled. (Genesis 6:5–6)

It seems that if God had fully utilized his omniscience, he would not have been surprised to discover the full extent of man's wickedness in the earth. Yet this passage clearly states that God regretted making human beings in light of their detestable actions and wicked hearts.

For God to allow himself to be all-knowing all the time means that while he is thinking about the work of Christ on the cross or his love for you, he is also thinking about every way in which evil possibly could be concocted. Although theoretically God could know all things, Scripture clearly indicates that he doesn't, especially as it relates to man's exercise of free will. Time and time again, God limited himself in favor of granting man full access to personal freedom.

Again, the correct interpretation of sovereignty has nothing to do with an entity "controlling everything." Yet despite this term's lack of usage in Scripture, this extreme sovereignty of God doctrine continues to be used unashamedly in religious circles the world over to define the nature and character of God.

As long as God's character and actions seem impulsive, abrupt, and beyond our understanding, we will never be able to maintain confidence in approaching him.

THE PROBLEM OF EVIL

While the sovereignty of God doctrine is popular in theological circles and in college lecture halls, it holds little water in everyday life. For whenever trouble hits close to home, notions of God's sovereign purpose might be uttered, but few people are actually comforted by it. In our hearts, we believe (or at least want to believe) that God is good but find it virtually impossible, as we should, to rationalize him as having a purpose behind or beyond our pain. Eventually, something has to give. Either we desensitize ourselves to the pain of the moment, reluctantly holding on to our theological position of "Everything happens for a reason," or we realize the absurdity of that belief and become angry with God for the pain we are told he is causing. We know that if God really is good, then he can't be allowing or causing evil in our lives.

> God is actually better than we have previously thought.

I mentioned earlier the countless hours I spent studying this very question, known as the problem of evil—"If God is good, then why does he allow bad things to happen?" This question has haunted philosophers and theologians for eons and has led countless people to falsely conclude that due to the evil in the world, God can't possibly be good.

I propose a new perspective. Because of the existence of evil, we can be convinced that God is actually better than we have previously thought.

Allow me to illustrate. A world where no evil exists is also a world absent from choice. It might be a cleaner world, but it would still be a world forced upon humankind and devoid of love—for love always gives a choice. John Haught writes,

> Love by its very nature can not compel, and so any God whose very essence is love should not be expected to overwhelm the world either with a coercively directive power or an annihilating presence. Indeed, an infinite love must in some ways absent or restrain itself, precisely in order to give the world the space in which to become something distinct from the creative love that constitutes it as other. We should anticipate, therefore, that any universe rooted in an unbounded love would have some features that appear to us as random and undirected.[6]

Through the act of creation, Haught contends, God willingly and purposefully gave up control of the universe in order to allow humankind to maintain our free will.

Bernard Haisch expounds further on Haught's words in his book *The God Theory*.

> Rather than pulling puppet strings, this deity voluntarily relinquishes control to its creatures so that new and autonomous things may arise. This enhances creation by bringing forth the unplanned, the unscripted, the random, the "other" that flows naturally from this act. . . .

The universe is thus invited to participate in its own crafting. This ongoing, participatory act of creation is, in fact, the ultimate expression of God's love.[7]

What a beautiful picture—God has invited us to participate in our own destiny! In his goodness, he refuses to force our hand, to make us love him, or to make us do what is right. He gives us the opportunity to choose. And to choose to follow him, to choose whether we will forgive those who hurt us—our participation is always needed.

CHAOS THEORY

It's important we realize that infinite factors accumulate in order to create our present reality. Everything does happen for a reason, but that doesn't mean God is behind each and every reason. To see all our situations as "God's plan" not only strips people of their responsibility to choose, but it also villainizes God and blames him for the bad circumstances we experience in this world. The negative experiences of our lives happen for a variety of reasons—however, none of those reasons has its origin in God.

In mathematics, chaos theory looks at the behavior of what are called dynamical systems, whereby minute changes in one system produce drastic differences in the outcomes of other systems. According to chaos theory, events in life are the result of small, seemingly insignificant human decisions, rather than the result of actions executed by some sort of cosmic or divine being. Perhaps some have heard of the popularized term from this field of study, "the butterfly effect," based on the idea that if a butterfly flaps its wings in New Mexico, that action could cause the weather to change in Chicago. Leaving the house five minutes later than planned can lead to a drastically different course of events throughout your day than if you had left on time.

Although physics doesn't usually comment on faith or God, its theories are not contradictory and the principles carry over. In this instance, science has demonstrated we have a role in our destiny—our choices affect not just ourselves but others. In fact, much of the pain of this life has human choice, not God, at its epicenter. But should this really surprise us? After all, wasn't it Genesis that first revealed God's intentions for us to rule over this world, only to have mankind eat the forbidden fruit and send us off on an orbit of choosing our own destiny, all the while blaming God for the fallout? Why do we now doubt that his will is any different? Or that our responses to this freedom would be any different? If God is at fault, it isn't for causing our pain but rather for giving us free choice.

EVERYTHING HAPPENS FOR A REASON

While the doctrine of extreme sovereignty leaves us with only two choices to describe the reasons for the various outcomes of this world (either God caused it or he allowed it—both putting the responsibility on God), in reality, one could infer at least five different yet plausible causes for why something happens in our lives. Let's consider for a moment all the possible causes for our circumstances:

1. God caused it.
2. Satan caused it.
3. I caused it.
4. Someone else caused it.
5. Natural circumstances caused it. (Weather patterns, laws of physics, earthquakes, etc.)

With so many plausible causes, why is it so easy to immediately blame God when adverse circumstances take place?

When I was around twelve years old, my older brother and I transformed our family room into a soccer field and used one of our younger sister's oversized teddy bears as a ball. It was the perfect size, and I suppose we assumed the soft, fluffy exterior would prevent the toy from doing much damage to the collectibles and picture frames lining the room. I don't remember the score at the time, but I do remember my brother kicking the head of that brown-and-white bear so hard it launched past my head and crashed into the fireplace mantle behind me. "Goal!" he yelled as the porcelain Lladro figurine, worth hundreds of dollars, fell through my fingertips and shattered into a million pieces against the brick fireplace. Needless to say, teddy-bear soccer was only fun while it lasted.

If I remember correctly, my brother took the blame for my goalie error, but it didn't change the fact that our parents were angry. Now imagine for a moment that, instead of recognizing the exclusive role our actions played in this event, my brother and I said, "I'm sorry that this happened, Mom and Dad, but we know that God must have allowed it for a reason." Hmm . . . probably not the smart-aleck tone you'd want to take after just obliterating Mom's family heirloom. And it goes without saying that offering this explanation would only have placed us in more hot water than we already were, since everyone knew it was our fault. But as luck would have it, because we took responsibility for our actions, we walked away with just a verbal lashing.

The reality is that the doctrine of extreme sovereignty is birthed out of convenience. If everything that happens is God's will, then it's easy to divert the attention off our personal shortcomings and chalk them up to God's master plan. "God knew that the only way that I would ever change is if I went through a divorce." "God took my job away because he wanted to teach me how to trust him with my finances." "I should have been cast in that new movie. I was really the best one for the part, but God has better things in store for me."

According to this doctrine, if things work, then it was God's will; and if they don't work, well, then, that was God's will too. As one eighteenth-century poet wrote, "One truth is clear. Whatever is, is right."[8]

PERSONAL RESPONSIBILITY

The doctrine of sovereignty provides a convenient escape from personal responsibility, for if God is always seen as in control of every event in the world—then *I* am not. And while there are things in this world that are beyond my control, there is much that is not. It's clear humanity would rather blame God for the evils of this world than take responsibility. Yet if we are to welcome the goodness of God, then we have no choice but to embrace personal responsibility. I play a part in my life. My choices have consequences. The bad things that erupt out of my actions come not from God's will but rather from my freedom to choose—including the freedom to make the wrong choice.

For God, though, the responsibility and ultimate reign on this earth he granted to man and woman was never designed to place blame on them or assign them fault. God bestowed humankind with responsibility as a way of empowering us to rule this world in any way we see fit and reminding us that we have a vote to cast in the ballot of our lives. As the psalmist adds, "The highest heavens belong to the LORD, but the earth he has given to mankind" (Psalm 115:16).

Our actions affect our lives. This answer is too simple for some, but it's the truth—God has granted men and women imminent domain over their own choices. In fact, not even the devil can make us do something. The final authority of our personal choice lies in our hands. This fact can empower us to bring about tremendous good in the world, or we can hide from personal responsibility and remain victims.

Some might hear this and assume responsibility implies fault. Fault ascribes the causation of the problem to a specific person, and although there are certainly times where this is the case (for example, when someone commits a crime or starts an argument), there are plenty of other times (as in the miscarriage of our child or my wife's need for open-heart surgery) that are not a result of human choice at all and therefore specific fault should never be ascribed. But in these instances should we give up and play the victim? I say no! Taking responsibility for our free will and the authority we have in Christ should empower us to rise above every circumstance and to overcome in this world. As John writes, "Who is it that overcomes the world? Only the one who believes that Jesus is the Son of God" (1 John 5:5).

Of course, with the freedom to choose right, we also possess the ability to choose wrong, giving birth to untold hurt and pain in our lives and in the lives of those around us. As Paul states, "Those who live according to the flesh have their minds set on what the flesh desires; but those who live in accordance with the Spirit have their minds set on what the Spirit desires. The mind governed by the flesh is death, but the mind governed by the Spirit is life and peace. The mind governed by the flesh is hostile to God; *it does not submit to God's law, nor can it do so*" (Romans 8:5–7).

If the extreme sovereignty doctrine were true, then Paul would not have added, "It does not submit to God's law, nor can it do so." For if God is in control, as the doctrine of sovereignty teaches, then even the sinful mind would have to submit to God's law. But this isn't the case. God in his goodness never forces people to change their minds—it's always our choice.

THE OTHER PERSON

"It was supposed to be a safe place," my friend confided in me, referring to growing up in church. As a young boy in a rural community, he often found himself alone with a family friend at inopportune times. "I didn't understand what was happening. I trusted this man, but I knew something was wrong," he continued, holding back tears. As I've listened to him, and many others, tell their heartbreaking stories of childhood sexual or physical abuse, I have come to realize that the guilt and confusion that follow such an offense can be just as damaging as the event itself. Victims of abuse and other traumatic experiences are often plagued by a barrage of questions, most notably, "Why would God allow this to happen?"

Sadly, the "everything happens for a reason" exploiters have further damaged hurting people by encouraging them to ask God what he could be trying to teach them through this suffering, or worse yet, blaming the victims for their part in causing these crimes to happen in the first place. Take, for instance, victims of rape. A prevailing thought once existed among men and women alike that if a woman was raped, it must have been because she was dressed a certain way or because she acted in a way that drew that attention to herself. In our desperate attempt to find an answer to, "Why did this happen?" people became willing to blame even the victim in order to rationalize and make sense of the experience.

Thankfully, social causes advancing the rights of women have reversed some of that thinking, and victims of rape and other forms of abuse are now encouraged to understand that the abuse was *not* their fault. The real truth is that abuse and domestic violence exist because psychotic people *choose* to perpetrate these heinous crimes.

Regrettably, the rationale of many in the church has barely evolved beyond the aforementioned attitude. Christians even proudly claim such bad circumstances happen so that victims can eventually use their testimony to help others. Think for a moment about what people are actually saying in these types of statements: either God is so focused on helping *others* that he's willing to hurt *you* in order to do it, or worse yet, God is more interested in promoting *himself* (allowing this for his glory), than he is in caring for the safety of his children. It's no wonder that so many have fled from the church as misinformed notions like these thoughtlessly drip from the mouths of naive congregants and clergy.

There's no doubt that the "Everything happens for a reason" belief system stems, in part, from a well-known passage in the gospel of John, which records a story about a man who was born blind (John 9:1–11). Jesus' disciples, like so many today, were trying to fathom the *reason* for the man's suffering. "Jesus, *why* was this man born blind?" they essentially asked. They thought this man's blindness must have been a form of punishment. "Who sinned, this man or his parents, that he was born blind?" they asked Jesus (John 9:2). And with a compassion that only Jesus could offer, he responds simply with, "Neither."

Many have struggled with this passage, because in the verses that follow, due to issues with punctuation in the text, Jesus seems to suggest that the man's blindness was indeed purposed so that God might have the opportunity to heal the man. Eugene Peterson, however, in his masterful paraphrase of the Bible, demonstrates the proper sentiment behind this passage.

> Jesus said, "*You're asking the wrong question. You're look-ing for someone to blame. There is no such cause-effect here.* Look instead for what God can do. We need to be energetically at work for the One who sent me here, working while the sun shines. When night falls, the workday is over. For as long as I am in the world, there is plenty of light. I am the world's Light." (John 9:3–5 MSG)

When you begin to realize God is truly good all the time, you will discover suffering is *never* for a specific God-ordained purpose (i.e., God allowed our suffering so that something else good could come out of it). When suffering takes place, we need to "look instead for what God can do." Although Peterson's view on this passage, and the subsequent realization that God is not in the suffering business, is clearly in opposition to the popular stance on the redemptive purpose of suffering, it's the only viewpoint we can take if we are serious about seeing God as truly good. For God to play any part in our suffering other than Comforter, Healer, Deliverer, and so forth is to remove all elements of his goodness.

> **When you begin to realize God is truly good all the time, you will discover suffering is *never* for a specific God-ordained purpose.**

Is suffering redemptive? No. But because we suffer, God redeems us.

"ACTS OF GOD"

In the aftermath of Hurricane Katrina, perhaps the most destructive hurricane ever to hit the coastal United States, one of the most famous pastors of the last century was asked in a TV interview why God would allow such devastation to come on the people of New Orleans. This pastor shook his head and admitted that he didn't know—in fact, he had been wondering the same thing.

"He didn't do it!" I shouted from my living room. "God loves the people of New Orleans, and Jesus died for their sins too! This wasn't his will, and he had nothing to do with it. But since it happened, now is the time for the church to rise up and show these hurting families God's love and grace! Let's go help the people of New Orleans!" For me, this would have been a perfect opportunity to reveal to the world the true character and nature of God. Instead, America heard silence in this highly respected minister's answer. To those still listening, his answer gave the impression that God was to blame and that his reasons for flooding the Gulf Coast were beyond our comprehension.

Of course, this attitude about God doesn't just stop at him allowing hurricanes. Over the years, I've heard God blamed for everything from shark attacks and sinkholes to brain tumors. Regarding which, F. F. Bosworth writes in his classic book *Christ the Healer*: "If the modern theology of those who teach that God wants some of His worshippers to remain sick for His glory is true, then Jesus, during His earthly ministry, never hesitated to rob the Father of all the glory He could by healing *all* who came to Him."[9]

I believe the same can be said for the winds and the waves that Jesus rebuked in the Gospels (Matthew 8:26; Mark 4:39; Luke 8:24). If these natural occurrences were a result of God's will, then for Jesus to calm the storm would be for him to defy the purposes of God and to commit divine treason.

Natural disasters are a byproduct of the laws of nature. Typhoons, hurricanes, and tornados are the result of clashing weather patterns. Tsunamis are the result of underwater earthquakes. These events are often random, though some are predictable by season, geography, and atmospheric conditions. For example, my sister and her husband recently moved to Oklahoma. There less than a year, they've already experienced a tornado, a small earthquake, a forest fire, and a couple of poisonous snakes in their yard. Does God hate Oklahoma? I don't think so. It just so happens that this part of the country is prone to such natural occurrences, due to the weather patterns and other geophysical conditions.

Some might argue, though, that Scripture specifies several natural events and disasters that were sent from the hand of God—and I would agree. The great flood waters of Noah (Genesis 7:24), the shaking of Mount Sinai (Exodus 19:18), the sinkhole that swallowed Korah and his men (Numbers 16:31–32), and even the large fish that devoured Jonah (Jonah 1:17) were all the result of God's direction and authority. So am I saying that God has changed? Absolutely not. But God did change us!

Christ ushered in a new world order, if you will—where righteousness could be gained by faith instead of the law and the wrath of God would be satisfied through the sacrifice of the Son. Under the Old Covenant, sin was met with wrath and judgment. But now, under the New Covenant, grace and mercy reign supreme. This differentiation between Old and New is perhaps best illustrated by Jesus' response to the rejection he experienced in the Samaritan village in Luke 9:51–56.

> As the time approached for him to be taken up to heaven, Jesus resolutely set out for Jerusalem. And he sent messengers on ahead, who went into a Samaritan village to get things ready for him; but the people there did not welcome him, because he was heading for Jerusalem. When the disciples James and John saw this, they asked, "Lord, do you want us to call fire down from heaven to destroy them?" But Jesus turned and rebuked them. Then he and his disciples went to another village.

Calling down fire from heaven to consume your haters may sound a little extreme in today's world, but in Old Testament times, acts like these were commonplace. Take for example the story of the prophet who summoned two bears out of the woods to devour forty-two teens who made fun of his bald head (2 Kings 2:23–25). But here in Luke, Jesus responds differently—instead of granting his disciples' request, he *rebuked* their methods; revealing God's true attitude of grace and mercy.

Despite being the source of all life, power, and glory that could ever exist, God does not always get what he wants. A quick survey of Scripture verifies this fact. Mankind ate the forbidden fruit against his will (Genesis 2:17). King Saul failed to keep the commands of God, forcing God to choose another to take his place (1 Samuel 13:13). God is not willing that any perish (2 Peter 3:9), yet we know that some will. And the list goes on and on. How hard it must be for God to know what is best for his creation yet watch with a heavy heart as we continue to make choices that take us away from the path he truly desires for us.

Laying down the extreme sovereignty of God doctrine is a fully liberating experience. It allows us to see the world the way God intended and introduces us to our rights and privileges as children of God. Most of all, by embracing my own personal authority over my choices and recognizing the role that others' actions and happenstance play in my life, I am able to recognize that God is not the source of my problems. What's more, I am able to once again see God as he is—a good, loving, and caring Father who desires only the best for his children. When bad things happen, I now never have to wonder if God is at the root of my pain. Instead, I can walk in the understanding that he loves me.

CHAPTER FOUR

THE MAN BEHIND THE CURTAIN

The Hallmark God

OVER A CUP OF COFFEE at a local café, my friend blurted out, "I feel like Job." A passionate Christian, he shared with me that he and his wife had been struggling with infertility. After the pain and disappointment of two miscarriages, my friend admitted he was mad at God and said if he wasn't afraid of going to hell, he probably would have given up his faith months ago.

"God had the power to save our babies, right? So why didn't he?" he inquired. "How am I supposed to trust someone after he just allowed two of my kids to die?" He surprised even himself at the boldness with which the words left his mouth.

Like my friend, an incalculable number of individuals, myself included, have faced nearly insurmountable hardships that beg the question, "Why, God?" Not surprisingly, in an attempt to make sense of any situation we can't understand, we've created Hallmark-like theologies and catchall phrases, almost all wrongly concluded from the book of Job. Here are just a few:

- "God is in control."
- "Everything happens for a reason."
- "I think God is testing me."
- "God might close a door, but he always opens a window."
- "God needed another angel in heaven."
- "You just have to let go and let God."
- "His ways are higher than our ways."
- "If it doesn't kill you, it will make you stronger."
- "If God leads you to it, he'll bring you through it."
- "Don't worry; God is always on time."
- "God will turn your test into your testimony."
- "Suffering is just a blessing in disguise."

Do any of these statements sound familiar? If you've ever been through a tragedy, then they probably do. Of course, these clichés are intended to make us feel better, but they inevitably leave us wanting more. For those who are truly searching for answers from a God who is supposed to be good, we can all agree that these trite sayings offered up to us by well-intentioned people are not enough to satisfy the hunger of a soul yearning to find answers, a heart longing to know the truth.

Furthermore, the Bible, the very tool we have been given to

gain knowledge and insight regarding the true nature of God, offers us little comfort or relief after going through the wringer of twisted religious commentary. Consider Charles Spurgeon, renowned nineteenth-century theologian, who offers his view of why suffering exists:

> One answer, doubtless, is, that God knows what is for his own glory, and that he giveth no account of his matters; that having permitted free agency, and having allowed, for some mysterious reason, the existence of evil, it does not seem agreeable with his having done so to destroy Satan; *but he gives him power that it may be a fair hand-to-hand fight between sin and holiness*, between grace and craftiness. Besides, be it remembered, that incidentally *the temptations of Satan are of service to the people of God*; Fenelon says they are the file which rubs off much of the rust of self-confidence, and I may add, they are the horrible sound in the sentinel's ear, which is sure to keep him awake. An experimental divine remarks, that there is no temptation in the world which is so bad as not being tempted at all; for to be tempted will tend to keep us awake: whereas, being without temptation, flesh and blood are weak—and though the spirit may be willing, yet we may be found falling into slumber. *Children do not run away from their father's side when big dogs bark at them. The howlings of the devil may tend to drive us nearer*

to Christ, may teach us our own weakness, may keep us upon our own watch-tower, and be made the means of preservation from other ills.[1]

Although Spurgeon admits he cannot fully comprehend the existence of evil, he concludes that since evil exists, God must have wanted it to. Furthermore, he states that we wouldn't really be living if we weren't being tempted. Lastly, he determines that if God's love is not enough to keep his children close by his side, then he apparently has no qualms about employing Satan to scare his children into not leaving him. For those wishing to wade past the dark waters of deep suffering and safely reach the opposite shore of God's unconditional love, we must push beyond these conventional commentaries and find refuge in the revealing light of God's Word.

PAY NO ATTENTION

You might remember in the classic 1939 movie *The Wizard of Oz* the scene in which Dorothy and her friends stood trembling with fear after delivering the Wicked Witch's broomstick to the Wizard of Oz. Unbeknownst to the group, faithful Toto slipped away and began tugging on a large curtain in the corner of the room. Toto pulled back the curtain to reveal a man frantically pushing and pulling levers and buttons on a control panel and speaking into a microphone. Embarrassed that his cover had been blown, the man leaned into the microphone and pleaded,

"Pay no attention to that man behind the curtain!" But it was too late.

"Who are you?" Dorothy asked, pulling aside the curtain. "Are *you* the Wizard of Oz?" she muttered in disbelief. Indeed, the great and powerful Wizard of Oz was simply a trickster in disguise, using ingenuity and sleight of hand to pull off the greatest con the Land of Oz had ever seen. Finally, the Lion, the Tin Man, the Scarecrow, Dorothy, and her little dog too, stood in amazement before a man who had once sent chills of fear down their spines and caused them to embark on a perilous journey to help Dorothy find her way home.

Ironically, Satan differs little from the Wizard of Oz character in this 1939 movie. Having been defeated at the cross and stripped of the authority he once maintained, he now hides behind a curtain of deception, pulling the levers of suffering, punching the buttons of strife, trying to make us think not only that he is a great and powerful match to God but that our good God collaborates with him to test his precious children. Satan's goal is for us to focus our attention on his distorted version of God, and all the while he whispers in our ear, "Pay no attention to that man behind the curtain." In the words of French poet Charles Pierre Baudelaire, "the loveliest trick of the Devil is to persuade you that he does not exist."[2]

The Bible speaks prophetically of the final day when Satan's curtain of deception will be once and for all pulled to the side, and we will see him for who he truly is:

How art thou fallen from heaven, O Lucifer, son of the morning! how art thou cut down to the ground, which didst weaken the nations!

They that see thee shall narrowly look upon thee, and consider thee, saying, Is this the man that made the earth to tremble, that did shake kingdoms;

That made the world as a wilderness, and destroyed the cities thereof; that opened not the house of his prisoners? (Isaiah 14:12, 16–17 KJV)

Much like Dorothy's response to the Wizard of Oz, on that last day the world will gaze with disbelief at the enemy and say, "Is *this* the one?" Not only will people be shocked that they were ever afraid of Satan, but they will be dumbfounded that Satan so effortlessly led people away from the true heart of God.

PULLING BACK THE CURTAIN

Before we pull back the curtain on Satan's deception promulgated through the book of Job, we must first establish a few key facts. Historically, the book of Job is one of the oldest stories in Scripture. Many Bible scholars estimate these events occurred *prior* to the life of the patriarch Abraham.[3] So the story of Job chronologically takes place somewhere between Genesis 4 and Genesis 11. This historical dating of Job is crucial to our understanding of the events that transpire in the book, primarily as they relate to the condition in which we find Satan. Allow me to explain.

Since Lucifer is a created being, he must gain knowledge and understanding (about mankind, the world in which we live, and even about God and God's ways) through learning, much like you and I do. For example, the Bible reveals that if Satan had known what Jesus' death on the cross had meant, he never would have crucified Jesus (1 Corinthians 2:8). That is a profound reality. To Christians, the story of the cross is clear—at least in retrospect. But at the time, the Bible says Satan had no concept that by killing the Son of God, his own destruction would ensue and his captives would be forever set free. If Satan had realized that the death of Christ would free mankind from his grips, he would have done everything in his power to try to prevent it.

This also means that the knowledge and understanding Satan had in the Garden after the Fall was *limited* in scope compared to the awareness Satan now possesses two thousand years later. By no means am I implying that Satan is dumb or unintelligent. I'm simply suggesting that the Lucifer whom we met in the account of the Garden is not the same Lucifer we encounter throughout the rest of the Bible, or even today, for that matter. Unlike God, Satan changes, shifts tactics, and learns by observation or through trial and error.

What follows is that Satan's appearance in the story of Job

occurred *only several generations* after his acquisition of Adam and Eve's power and authority at the Fall. Remember, when Adam and Eve gave in to Lucifer's temptation, they signed over co-ownership of their lease upon this earth and became guilty of the same crime as Lucifer—rebellion (1 John 5:19). As a result, Satan usurped mankind's authority over the earth, authority he exercised freely until Christ "disarmed" him at the cross (Colossians 2:15), thus ending Satan's regime.

Like the great and powerful Wizard of Oz, Satan would like nothing more than for us to believe that his power remains intact and that God is the source of our problems. We must pull back this curtain of deceit, however, and show the world that God really is good—in every sense of the word. In order to do so, however, we'll need to tackle what I call the Job Conspiracy, for as long as we think that God is the source of our problems, we'll never be able to trust his intentions.

THE JOB CONSPIRACY

Probably the most troubling passages from the book of Job transpire in chapters 1 and 2. These chapters describe an interaction between God and Satan that Christian tradition interprets much like this: God recommends that Satan take notice of his very good and holy servant Job, and when Satan agrees to this recommendation by saying, "Hey, yeah, that's a great idea. Remove your hand of protection so I can get him," God says, "Okay, I give in. Take all that he has. Just don't harm him."

With a theology like this, is it any wonder so many have been turned off by the church? Should we be surprised when our friends and loved ones want nothing to do with the God we preach? Even prior to understanding God's goodness, I always struggled with understanding the first chapter of Job. It just didn't seem to line up with the rest of Scripture. Why would God and Satan team up to test Job? Did they? Why would God recommend that Satan tempt Job? Did he? The answer to these questions set me free from years of distrust toward God and allowed me to see him as he truly is. Let's examine these passages further.

> As long as we think that God is the source of our problems, we'll never be able to trust his intentions.

WHAT'S IN A WORD?

In Job 1:7–12, Satan presents himself before God, God asks Satan where he has come from, and Satan replies, "From roaming throughout the earth, going back and forth on it" (v. 7). God follows up with a perplexing question: "Have you considered my servant Job?" (v. 8). Next Satan retorts, "Stretch out your hand and strike everything he has, and he will surely curse you to your face" (v. 11). So God concludes with, "Very well, then, everything he has is in your power, but on the man himself do not lay a finger" (v. 12).

Based on the common interpretation of this passage, most Christians believe that the first chapter of Job goes a little something like this: Imagine the neighborhood bully ringing your doorbell. Wondering what he's up to now, you answer, "Well, hello, Butch. What are you doing here?"

"I'm bored and I've been riding my bike around, looking for someone to beat up," says Butch.

You promptly respond, "Have you considered my son, Johnny? He's quite an amazing kid. There's really no one like him in this entire neighborhood."

"Oh yeah? I'll show you what he's really like. If you let me steal everything from his room, I bet he'll curse you!"

"Okay, try it!" you energetically offer up.

Now, I'm pretty sure if this incident transpired on your doorstep, not only would you have some choice words for Butch, but you'd also have a few suggestions for Johnny should he ever be bothered by Butch when you're not around. This scenario might make for a good movie scene, but you'd be hard-pressed to find any parent in your circle employing this tactic to showcase his or her child's character.

Yet this is the most common interpretation of the events in chapter 1 of Job. Never mind that Scripture teaches that God does not willingly bring grief or affliction to the sons of men (Lamentations 3:33), that God tells us to cast all our anxiety on him because he cares for us (1 Peter 5:7), that the Lord will rescue us from every evil attack and will bring us safely to his heavenly kingdom (2 Timothy 4:18), and so on. Somehow, in the context of the book of Job, Christians have thrown out everything they know about God's love made manifest to humanity in the person of Jesus Christ and have invented a god who exists only within the confines of their twisted religious tradition!

So if God is not suggesting that Satan test Job, then what exactly *is* he saying? Let's take a closer look at the Hebrew word for "considered" in verse 8—"Have you *considered* my servant Job?" The word "considered" in Hebrew means "to set your heart upon."[4] Therefore, a more proper reading of God's question in verse 8 would be, "Have you *set your heart upon* my servant Job?" You see, God wasn't acquiescing to Satan's suggestion, offering up Job like a prisoner in a gladiator's ring. God was actually *accusing* Satan of considering harming Job! Like a father witnessing his teenage daughter being ogled by a stranger, God was calling out Satan for his intentional glances in the direction of his favorite child, *not* suggesting that the devil attack him.

God's response to Satan roaming around, seeking whom he may devour (1 Peter 5:8), was more like, "What have you been doing? Have you set your evil intentions upon Job? Are you considering harming him? There is no one on earth like him. Do *not* lay a finger on him!" This subtle difference creates a drastic theological inversion. Rather than impugning God's character, this passage actually glorifies his goodness and reveals God's intention and the true nature of his question.

The next troubling passage appears in verses 11 and 12 of Job chapter 1. In these verses, typical Christian doctrine would have us believe that because of the way God responded to Satan's suggestion ("Very well, then, everything he has is in your hands" [v. 12]), Satan is somehow a formidable foe to God. Apparently Bible scholars think that Satan is able to convince God not only to remove his hand of protection from Job but also to allow Satan to be God's agent of destruction to strike down everything Job had.

Now, before we consider this passage in its original language, we must admit that the most widely accepted theology of Job goes something like this: *Satan tempts God to withhold his hand of protection from Job, God gives in, then God teams up with Satan to inflict hardship on Job.* How can this be when James tells us, "God cannot be tempted by evil, nor does he tempt anyone" (James 1:13)? Based on this verse alone it should be *impossible* for us to conclude that Satan was able to talk God into allowing him to harm Job.

Let's look at this passage more carefully. To begin with, the word translated "Very well, then" (Job 1:12) is also translated "behold" in the King James Version. It is the Hebrew word *hinneh*. Recently I was discussing this word with a friend of mine who holds a PhD in Hebrew and Judaic Studies from the

University of Toronto. He offered from his studies that "very well, then" is a rather poor translation of the Hebrew word *hinneh*. "Believe it or not," he said, "*hinneh* is much closer to *presto!* or *check it out*!" He added, "*Hinneh* is a word that enacts a change of perspective, moving the reader or addressee to see momentarily from the vantage point of the speaker. In this case, God is showing Satan God's own perspective."

So what does that mean in light of this passage? God's words to Satan in Job 1:12 ("Very well, then, everything he has is in your power") are not bestowing divine authority upon the devil to harm Job, or even God *allowing* Satan to do his bidding. Rather, this statement is an acknowledgment by God of the present condition of the situation—the truth of the matter. *Presto!* Like a magician pulling back the curtain to reveal the reality of a situation, the Hebrew word *hinneh* used here implies that God is simply presenting to the enemy the current state of affairs from God's own perspective. After all, God cannot lie, and therefore he is obliged to tell the truth, even if it means revealing to Satan the extent of his newfound power and authority. In this case, God is simply stating, "Look, you're the one with the gun. You usurped mankind's authority decades ago. For now, you have legal right to act upon this earth."

HE GIVES AND TAKES AWAY

A friend of mine once described the internal dilemma he was facing like this: "I've never been able to shake myself of the idea that God is my problem. I feel like my life would have been easier if I could have, though." Job was no different. Although Satan seized the authority afforded to him after the Fall and attacked all that Job had, Job had no concept that Satan even existed. In response to who possibly could have incited such evil against him, Job asks in a most telling voice, "If it is not [God], then who is it?" (9:24). The idea that his problems have come as a result of an adversary never crosses Job's mind.

Isn't it interesting that thousands of years later, just like Job and his friends, Christians draw the same conclusions about God even to this day? A loss of employment? God must be redirecting our calling. Cancer? A blessing in disguise. Fatal car accident? One of God's ways to call his children home.

Plagued with the false notion that God allows everything in our lives, people rarely consider that another power is at work. How disturbing that these thoughts come from the very people who are shaping the Christian culture and beliefs of our time.

In the latter part of the book of Job, Job's friends (having already mistakenly concluded that God is responsible for Job's plight) debate whether Job *deserves* the punishment they assume God had inflicted. Job is under the impression that his good deeds are enough to guarantee his righteousness apart from faith. As a result, he sees his suffering as unjust and blames God for it. His friends, on the other hand, apparently tired of Job's constant defensiveness and pride, plead with him, "When will you end these speeches? Be sensible, and then we can talk"

(18:2). They assert that Job must have done something for God to have unleashed his wrath upon him.

Consequently, after chapter upon chapter of Job's self-righteous "I don't deserve this. I'm a righteous man" garble, and his friends' "Is not your wickedness great? Are not your sins endless?" indictments (22:5), God finally shows up to settle the score once and for all and give Job exactly what he requested—a supernatural hearing in God's court of law (13:3).

So what is God's conclusion regarding what Job and his friends have been claiming? Who is right? Job or his friends? The short answer is—neither!

After warning Job to "Brace yourself like a man" (38:3), God responds to these accusations with, "Who is this that obscures my plans with words without knowledge? . . . I am angry with you and your two friends, because you have not spoken the truth about me. . . . Would you condemn me to justify yourself?" (38:2; 42:7; 40:8). God rebukes Job and his friends not only for their lack of understanding regarding the events that transpired but also for speaking what is untrue of him. What that means is that Christian tradition's popular "God allowed it" doctrines—derived primarily from passages in Job such as "The LORD gave and the LORD has taken away" (1:21) or "he injures, but his hands also heal" (5:18)—were refuted by God at the end of the book as being untrue.

Job himself sheepishly acknowledges this in chapter 42: "Surely I spoke of things I did not understand, things too wonderful for me to know. . . . My ears had heard of you but now my eyes have seen you. Therefore I . . . repent" (vv. 3–6). At last, with clarity of vision, Job finally sees God for the good God he truly is.

Since we have never been able to see God as anything but the sovereign perpetrator of all of our circumstances, we are incapable of seeing him for who he truly is. We've heard of God. We've read about God. But we don't know really know him. Why not? Because, like Job, our minds are constantly trying to harmonize what we know about God's mercy and grace with the negative circumstances we believe he allows. If God rebuked Job for speaking falsely about him, then let us not be duped into drawing the same conclusions.

DOUBLE FOR YOUR TROUBLE

Unfortunately, for centuries Christians have mistakenly concluded that the book of Job is about God's testing and Job's faithfulness. Since God eventually restored to Job all of his possessions (Job 42:10, 12), Christian doctrine has taught us that to remain faithful to God means to hold fast to him in spite of the hardships he allows. Without realizing the implications of this belief, Christians have been taught to embrace a self-righteous attitude that states, "Even though God allows bad things to happen to me, no matter what, *I* will still love him. *I* will still trust him. *I* will still serve him. *I* will still believe in him." In essence, most Christians have deemed themselves to be more faithful to God than he is to us.

Ironically, the idea that God was testing Job's faithfulness was *never* concluded by Job or his friends. Job and his friends didn't have a "Let's wait and see what this is all about" attitude. Rather, because of the circumstances that transpired, they determined that God had already issued his righteous judgment against Job, having found him guilty of sinning against the Lord. Furthermore, to conclude that Job was restored back into good graces with God because of his faithfulness hardly lines up with Scripture.

In the midst of Job's hardship, we never read about Job proclaiming, "God, even though you are allowing these trials, I choose to love you in spite of it!" And how could there be any room in his heart for love anyway when he was scared to death that God was on the verge of ending his life? With regard to trust, Job showed absolutely no signs of trusting that God would turn things around for the better. In fact, on multiple occasions, Job wanted to commit suicide because he was convinced his life was over. And Job certainly didn't continue serving God during his affliction; rather, he commiserated

> If God rebuked Job for speaking falsely about him, then let us not be duped into drawing the same conclusions.

with his friends and complained about why God had done this to him. And belief in God? What Job believed about God was that God was more likely to crush him with a storm or overwhelm him with misery than to restore his life for some divine purpose.

While it's true that Job finally put his hope back in the goodness of God, it wasn't without a stern rebuke from the Lord regarding all the things Job had *misspoken* about him. Yet because of God's goodness, God blessed the latter half of Job's life more than the first and took what the enemy intended for evil and turned it around for good. And as for the purpose behind Job's suffering? Quite frankly, there was no other purpose other than the enemy's desire to steal, kill, and destroy (John 10:10). God did not ordain Job's testing through the use of Satan. He was not coerced into allowing the enemy to take all that Job had. And he didn't need to inflict hardship on Job to see if he would remain faithful. Those are simply not God's ways.

As we humbly lay aside foolish theologies and stop allowing the enemy to cause us to question the goodness of God, we are now ready to tackle some of the most challenging passages in Scripture regarding God's use of discipline and testing.

CHAPTER FIVE

WISDOM AND FOOLISHNESS

The School of Hard Knocks

JOE SUFFERED FROM a painful hereditary condition. His grandfather had it, his father had it, and now he feared that his son would suffer the same fate. In many ways, this medical condition consumed his life. Prior to being diagnosed with this illness, Joe had lived a wild life of parties and substance abuse. However, as his ailment flared up, his rebellion settled down. Ironically, Joe was a Christian therapist, and after years of trying to utilize his practitioner's tools upon himself, he reached out to a mutual friend who referred Joe to me in hopes that I could lead him toward the healing he was so desperately looking for.

"Honestly, I'm thankful for my sickness," he said to me in one counseling session. "Who knows how messed up my life would have become if I had never gotten sick? I believe that

God gave me this disease to lead me back to him. It's made me who I am."

"So let me understand," I pushed back in hopes of making my point. "Even though you are a born-again believer, you think Christ, whom the Bible tells us 'took up our infirmities and bore our diseases' in Matthew 8:17, inflicted this illness on you to save you from your life of partying and that now your identity in Christ is defined by your sickness?"

"Well . . . no . . . but . . ." He stumbled to find words. "I guess I've never thought of it like that before." He sat there for a moment, clearly puzzled.

"All I know," he continued, "is that I just don't want to be sick anymore. I keep telling God, 'I've learned my lesson—can't I be done with this?'"

> **Many Christians suffer unnecessarily because they have been taught to embrace hardship as God's instruction or testing.**

As our sessions continued, Joe revealed his heart's true division about his illness. On the one hand, he recognized that his illness was not only affecting him physically but was also trapping him in emotional bondage because he felt guilty that he couldn't get healed. On the other hand, although his disease was killing him physically, he had developed a belief that this sickness had saved his life spiritually.

Over the course of the next several weeks, I met with Joe and showed him countless scriptures that detailed Jesus' attitude toward sickness and suffering (instruments of evil, not tools for shaping his children). Each time we met, I helped Joe let go of the false sense of identity he had established through his illness. In the end, when Joe finally embraced God's perspective of him and his illness (that God was not the source of his pain, nor did he delight in his disease), Joe's physical body was restored and he was free from his debilitating condition for the first time in almost two decades.

Like Joe, many Christians suffer unnecessarily because they have been taught to embrace hardship as God's instruction or testing. Christians have been foolishly told to praise God for their trials, including sickness and pain, and not to miss the lesson. Consider John Piper's words from his book *Don't Waste Your Cancer*:

> It will not do to say that God only uses our cancer but does not design it. What God permits, he permits for a reason. And that reason is his design. If God foresees molecular developments becoming cancer, he can stop it, or not. If he does not, he has a purpose. Since he is infinitely wise, it is right to call this purpose a design. . . . *If we don't believe our cancer is designed for us by God, we will waste it. . . .* That means the diseases we still bear are not a curse. They have been transformed from a punitive

pathway to hell into a purifying pathway to heaven. We are not cursed. As hard as it is to feel this, we believe God is not withholding good. He is doing good.[1]

Cancer is *God's* design? And as a result we shouldn't *waste* it? I find it sad that so many hold to this perspective about God.

This mind-set, however, is nothing new. For centuries humanity has wavered back and forth as to whether intellect or experience is responsible for knowledge. Today's pendulum has swung to the extreme of experience being our best teacher, and especially in Christian circles, the most widely held belief about God and his interactions with man is that God uses negative experiences in order to teach his children. Maybe that's why Jesus made a point to say in John 6:63: "The Spirit gives life; *the flesh counts for nothing.* The words I have spoken to you—they are full of the Spirit and life." You see, Jesus recognized that if we relate to God solely through our five physical senses, we will never receive the life we are looking for. Rather, if we listen to and apply God's *words* to our circumstances, only then can we find true life.

Unfortunately, like my friend Joe, most people who became closer to God after adverse circumstances conclude that God had to do something to get their attention, even if it meant allowing a life-threatening situation to overtake them. But let me ask you this question: If someone was totally unwilling to listen to the voice of God in his heart prior to a life-threatening circumstance, is it plausible that perhaps his lack of concern for God and his ways may have been a contributing factor in his suffering in the first place?

God forbid we take any responsibility for our choices or see the perpetrator of our suffering for who he really is. Scripture tells us that only a fool requires the school of hard knocks to learn (Proverbs 1:7), so why do Christians so wrongly and often conclude that God uses the "hard knocks" of suffering to teach his children? In short, our adversary, the devil, has convinced us once again to conclude that God uses discipline, testing, trials, and temptations to teach, train, and mature his children.

PAUL'S "THORN IN THE FLESH"

But didn't God give Paul a "thorn in [his] flesh" (2 Corinthians 12:7)? Isn't that an example of God using a hardship to shape and teach one of his children? The real answer might be a surprise to you.

In 2 Corinthians 12:6–10, Paul writes,

> Even if I should choose to boast, I would not be a fool, because I would be speaking the truth. But I refrain, so no one will think more of me than is warranted by what I do or say, or because of these surpassingly great revelations. Therefore, in order to keep me from becoming conceited, I was given a thorn in my flesh, a messenger of Satan, to torment me. Three times I pleaded with

the Lord to take it away from me. But he said to me, "My grace is sufficient for you, for my power is made perfect in weakness." Therefore I will boast all the more gladly about my weaknesses, so that Christ's power may rest on me. That is why, for Christ's sake, I delight in weaknesses, in insults, in hardships, in persecutions, in difficulties. For when I am weak, then I am strong.

Contrary to what you may have been taught, Paul identifies the source of his thorn in verse 7, and it didn't come from God! He calls the thorn a "messenger of Satan" sent to "torment" him. Does this sound like something that is from God? Additionally, many have been taught that this thorn was a type of sickness that was afflicting Paul. But he specifically tells us that the "thorn" is a "messenger." Everywhere Paul went, it seems Satan would send people to torment Paul and to stir up trouble for him, such as the demon-possessed girl in Acts 16. Joshua uses a similar term when speaking to the leaders of Israel, warning them of the importance of driving out the pagan nations that surrounded Israel. If they fail to drive them out, he says, they will become "whips on your backs and thorns in your eyes" (Joshua 23:13). Additionally, and perhaps most shockingly, is the real meaning of the Greek word translated "conceited" in 2 Corinthians 12:7. The Greek word *huperairó* means "to raise over."[2] The real reason behind Paul's thorn was that Satan was trying to prevent Paul from rising above his circumstances due to his revelation of God's goodness, therefore he sent the messenger to frustrate him.

Why was God unwilling to remove the thorn? Surprise again—he wasn't! In fact, God tells Paul exactly how to overcome it: through his grace! "My grace is sufficient," God says. Sufficient for what? For overcoming every attack and attempt from the enemy to keep us down.

TEMPTATION AND TESTING IN THE BOOK OF JAMES

James tells us, "Consider it pure joy, my brothers and sisters, whenever you face trials of many kinds, because you know that the testing of your faith produces perseverance" (James 1:2–3). This passage is often held as the quintessential perspective on suffering in Scripture. For centuries, Christian tradition has viewed testing as God's way of taking our faith to a higher level.

Regarding this passage, evangelist Billy Graham further expresses this opinion as he shares that God doesn't test us because *he* doesn't know how strong we are, but rather he tests us to show *us* how strong we really are. He adds,

> None of us likes to go through hard times (and God isn't necessarily behind them, even if He does allow them). But God can use them to show us our weaknesses. And when that happens, we need to ask God to help our faith grow. Testing should make us spiritually stronger—and it will as we turn it over to God.[3]

Though I applaud Reverend Graham for recognizing that God isn't behind every trial, his perspective does seem to fall into the commonly held belief that God is independently allowing specific trials into our lives for the purpose of growing us spiritually.[4] And to be honest, if all we read was James 1:2–3, I could see how one could come to this conclusion.

But what most people fail to recognize about this passage is that James goes on to define and clarify what should *not* be considered the source of our trials and temptations. He writes,

> *When tempted, no one should say, "God is tempting me."* For God cannot be tempted by evil, nor does he tempt anyone. . . . Don't be deceived, my dear brothers and sisters. Every good and perfect gift is from above, coming down from the Father of the heavenly lights, who does not change like shifting shadows. (James 1:13, 16–17)

It's important that we see the second verse in light of the whole passage, recognizing, like James, that God is not the source of our trials.

Perhaps even more disconcerting are some English translations of James's letter that attempt to create an unnecessary distinction between tests, trials, and temptations. In every instance in James 1:2–18, the words marked below in italics are the same Greek word, *peirasmos*, which is used interchangeably to describe what is translated in English as "test," "trial," or "temptation."[5] Consider James 1:2–3 and 12–15 in the New International Version:

> Consider it pure joy, my brothers and sisters, whenever you face *trials* of many kinds, because you know that the *testing* of your faith produces perseverance. . . .
>
> Blessed is the one who perseveres under *trial* because, having stood the *test*, that person will receive the crown of life that the Lord has promised to those who love him.
>
> When *tempted*, no one should say, "God is *tempting* me." For God cannot be *tempted* by evil, nor does he *tempt* anyone; but each person is *tempted* when they are dragged away by their own evil desire and enticed. Then, after desire has conceived, it gives birth to sin; and sin, when it is full-grown, gives birth to death.

No wonder so much confusion exists about God's goodness. Without recognizing the fact that James doesn't distinguish between trials, testing, or temptation, it's easy to question, "Does God give us trials, but not temptations?" "Does he test us, but not tempt us?"

This passage could be more accurately translated:

> Consider it pure joy, my brothers and sisters, whenever you face *trials, tests, or temptations* of many kinds,

because you know that the *testing, trying, or tempting* of your faith produces perseverance. . . .

Blessed is the one who perseveres under *trial, test, or temptation* because, having stood the *trial, test, or temptation*, that person will receive the crown of life that the Lord has promised to those who love him.

When *tried, tested, or tempted*, no one should say, "God is *trying, testing, or tempting* me." For God cannot be *tried, tested, or tempted* by evil, nor does he *try, test, or tempt* anyone; but each person is *tried, tested, or tempted* when they are dragged away by their own evil desire and enticed. Then, after desire has conceived, it gives birth to sin; and sin, when it is full-grown, gives birth to death.

Simply put, this passage could be paraphrased, "When trials and temptations come your way, it's an opportunity for your faith to shine! But don't be fooled into thinking that God is testing, trying, or tempting you—he's not. Only good gifts come from God."

This passage should encourage us that the trials we face do not possess the last word, and they certainly do not come from God. As James states, through patience, whether in this life or the next, we will "receive the crown of life that the Lord has promised to those who love him" (James 1:12). Although suffering is an opportunity to prove our faith, it does not presuppose that suffering comes from God's hand. In fact, I would argue the greatest reason for us to rejoice in and endure of suffering is that the trials we face are just one more opportunity for God to show himself strong on behalf of those whose hearts are faithful toward him.

A FATHER'S DISCIPLINE

In early November 2011, police responded to a South Bend family's home after neighbors reported screams emerging from the urban residence. Upon forced entry, officers discovered two boys bound with duct tape in the basement of the house. The younger brother, only ten years old, was already dead when the officers arrived. The older brother, fourteen at the time, was being forced to mop up his brother's blood when the police arrived. His body was covered with deep bruises and vicious wounds. The scene was described by one of the officers on-site as "one of the most horrendous crimes" he had seen.[6]

The boys' father, thirty-five-year-old Terry Sturgis, was sentenced to 140 years in prison for the death of his son and the physical abuse and torture of the other eight children who lived in the house. It was said that Terry used a club that night to kill his helpless son. One neighbor commented on the incident, saying, "I don't see anybody that angry to do that to their kids. How do you beat a child to death? How do you do that?"[7]

Like Sturgis's neighbor, most would agree that a crime like this is unthinkable—unfathomable. It doesn't even seem right to call it child abuse. It's worse than that. It's more like cold-blooded murder. There was no punishment, no lesson to be learned that could have deserved this sort of treatment or response, especially from a father.

Yet in the church, God is often portrayed as disciplining his children, even unto death. Sickness, deformity, and cancer are all referred to by religious groups as God's chastising—given to mature his children. How is it that Christians would condemn a man for abusing and eventually killing his son, but praise God for doing the same things in the lives of his own children? Some might ask, "But didn't God place Jesus on the cross? Why would we think we are exempt from physical discipline?" Unfortunately, such questions ignore the substitutionary work of the cross demonstrated through communion.

As a kid, growing up in a denomination that stressed the importance of weekly Communion, I was deathly afraid of 1 Corinthians 11:27–32, which states that improper use of Communion will cause a person to become "weak and sick" and may even be the reason that some have "fallen asleep" (a euphemism for "died"). To say the least, that's a cupful of discipline I was hoping to avoid! And the thought that I could accidentally take Communion in "an unworthy manner" by forgetting to acknowledge one of my weekly shortcomings frightened me enough to pass the plate more than once to avoid this spiritual snack time.

But later, upon discovering a fuller understanding of Jesus' work on the cross, I learned that it isn't God that is causing people to become "weak and sick," nor is it their technique in partaking of the bread and the juice. Instead, in verse 28, Paul explains that "everyone ought to examine themselves" before they partake and later in verse 29 that "those who eat and drink without discerning the body of Christ eat and drink judgment on themselves." So what does this mean? Paul is stating that when we receive Communion we should examine ourselves to see if we are in Christ. For the believer this should be a weekly reminder that we have been redeemed by the body and blood of Jesus. It should be a celebration of all that he has done, and never a fear of discipline or punishment! But by failing to see ourselves as recipients of Jesus' work on the cross, we remain under the curse and don't reap the benefits of our great salvation, which, among other things, includes healing. When I receive Communion now, instead of reciting this week's sin list, I praise God for my righteousness—that through Jesus' work on the cross, I've been redeemed: past, present, and future!

But 1 Corinthians 11 certainly isn't the only passage that has created confusion regarding the Lord's discipline. Perhaps the most questions about God's discipline come from Hebrews 12. This chapter is commonly used to place emphasis on God's supposed use of hardship to train us. In verses 4–11, the writer of Hebrews states,

> In your struggle against sin, you have not yet resisted
> to the point of shedding your blood. And have you

completely forgotten this *word of encouragement* that addresses you as a father addresses his son? It says,

"My son, do not make light of the Lord's discipline,
and do not lose heart when he *rebukes* you,
because the Lord disciplines the one he loves,
and he *chastens* everyone he accepts as
his son."

Endure hardship as discipline; God is treating you as his children. For what children are not disciplined by their father? If you are not disciplined—and everyone undergoes discipline—then you are not legitimate, not true sons and daughters at all. Moreover, we have all had human fathers who disciplined us and we respected them for it. *How much more should we submit to the Father of spirits and live!* They disciplined us for a little while as they thought best; but God disciplines us for our good, in order that we may share in his holiness. No discipline seems pleasant at the time, but painful. Later on, however, it produces a harvest of righteousness and peace for those who have been trained by it.

With a quick read, it would be easy to understand how this passage is used to claim that God may cause pain to his children for the purpose of confirming their sonship. Allow me to point out, however, a few commonly missed concepts regarding this passage.

To begin with, the writer starts by making an interesting statement regarding God's discipline, in that he calls it a "word of encouragement" (v. 5). Notice two things: first, God's discipline should be *encouraging*; and second, God's discipline is delivered in *words*. This is why the writer goes on to tell us not to "make light" of it (v. 5). For the religious minded, God's method of discipline involves sickness, trouble, or persecution. But if this were true, why would the writer need to tell us not to make light of it?

Losing your job isn't funny; neither are cancer, failed marriages, or car accidents. You can't ignore Parkinson's disease or domestic violence. But you can ignore someone's words. It's easy to make light of words—even God's. With words, we can choose to ignore them, refuse to obey them, or even to forget about them altogether. And with regard to God's Word, it's completely up to us whether we will take it seriously. Unfortunately, people ignore the words of God all the time.

Furthermore, the Greek word commonly used to describe discipline is *paideuó*, which means "to train up a child so they mature and realize their full potential."[8] Yet in English versions of the New Testament, *paideuó* is sometimes translated "punish" or "chastise," which readers commonly associate with considerably harsher connotations than the word contains (Hebrews 12:6; 1 Corinthians 11:32). Consider the word *paideuó* as it is used to describe Moses's high level of education while in Egypt in Acts 7:20–22:

> It was at this time that Moses was born; and he was lovely in the sight of God, and he was nurtured three months in his father's home. And after he had been set outside, Pharaoh's daughter took him away and nurtured him as her own son. Moses *was educated* [*paideuó*] in all the learning of the Egyptians, and he was a man of power in words and deeds. (NASB)

As an adopted member of Pharaoh's household, Moses was educated, not through the physical trials his Hebrew brothers and sisters went through outside the palace gates, but through the instruction of the wisest teachers in Egypt. He was nurtured by Pharaoh's daughter and likely carefully trained by the royal tutor. It is safe to assume that, like other Egyptian royalty, he would have been rigorously trained in astronomy, language, mathematics, and military strategy. The *paideuó*, or "training," that Moses received, and that Luke writes about in Acts, certainly may have been strenuous at times, but it would have been for the purpose of helping Moses realize his full potential, and consequently would have been delivered in wisdom-filled words, *not* harsh circumstances.

Likewise, in our culture, we use the word *discipline* to describe a wide array of activities, from spanking our children to the rigorous training that athletes undergo prior to a contest. The key factor, however, in distinguishing between discipline and abuse is the disposition of the one receiving the discipline. Discipline, as the New Testament writers understood it, was never an issue of force, anger, or violence. Instead, by nature discipline must be received by the one being chastised in order for it to be considered discipline in the first place.

Discipline is not an out-of-control paddling out of anger but an intentional training and shaping for the purpose of growing the character and nature of the person receiving it. With this in mind, spiritually speaking, what is often portrayed as God's discipline—sickness, cancer, and financial difficulty—rarely, if ever, offers us a choice prior to striking its blow.

Are we given a choice as to whether we want to be sick, an opportunity to say no to getting fired, or a chance to reject the hurricane prior to its making landfall on our shorelines? In any of these scenarios is there a metaphorical opportunity to bend over God's knee to receive our training? And even if there were, would we want to? Clearly not. For God to be at the source of such events would mean he is in fact punishing his children to the point of abuse, *not* disciplining them.

THE WORD OF GOD: SPIRITUAL BUMPER LANES

So then, if God, in his goodness, does not use hurricanes and cellular mutations to teach and train his people, what does he use? As we've already alluded to, according to Scripture God uses his Word to train us! Second Timothy 3:16–17 says, "All Scripture is God-breathed and is useful for teaching, rebuking, correcting and training in righteousness, so that the servant of God may be thoroughly equipped for every good work." God's Word, Paul tells Timothy, is his primary means of training and equipping his people.

For the believer, discipline is designed to be received from the Word of God. Ironically, though, this is often the last place we look. Don't believe me? Just scroll through your news feed on your favorite social media site. If yours is anything like mine, then between the pictures of painted toenails and homemade culinary creations are thankful philosophical musings about hardship and troubling times. Somewhere along the way, our hardships became forged into our identity. Why is this? Because we've confused godly discipline with hardship.

In Psalm 78, David shares the story of God's faithful deliverance of Israel, despite their continued stubborn rebellion and, at times, rejection of God's leading in their lives. It reads, "But they put God to the test and rebelled against the Most High; they did not keep his statutes. Like their ancestors they were disloyal and faithless, as unreliable as a faulty bow" (vv. 56–57). After all that God had done to deliver the people of Israel, they had every reason to follow God, but instead they rebelled against him, ignored his words, and justified their own behavior. As the writer of Hebrews recalls this, it should make sense why he felt compelled to remind his readers not to make light of the Lord's discipline. After all, it was their heritage.

Which is why it also is not surprising the author of the book of Hebrews wasn't the first to pen these words! In fact, in Hebrews 12:5–6, the writer is actually quoting Proverbs 3:11–12. In context, this quote further substantiates the fact that God uses words, not circumstances, to discipline his people. Take a quick look at the verses leading up to the quoted passage in Proverbs 3:1–12:

> My son, *do not forget my teaching*,
>   but *keep my commands* in your heart,
> for they will prolong your life many years
>   and bring you peace and prosperity.
>
> Let love and faithfulness never leave you;
>   bind them around your neck,
>   *write them on the tablet of your heart.*
> Then you will win favor and a good name
>   in the sight of God and man.
>
> Trust in the LORD with all your heart
>   and *lean not on your own understanding*;
> in all your ways submit to him,
>   and he will make your paths straight.

Do not be wise in your own eyes;
    fear the LORD and shun evil.
This will bring health to your body
    and nourishment to your bones.

Honor the LORD with your wealth,
    with the firstfruits of all your crops;
then your barns will be filled to overflowing,
    and your vats will brim over with new wine.

My son, *do not despise the LORD's discipline,*
    and do not resent his rebuke,
because the LORD disciplines those he loves,
    as a father the son he delights in.

Hopefully you can see that this entire passage in context is about words. Therefore, the writer urges us not to forget them, to keep them, to bind them, to write them on our hearts, to trust them, to submit to them, and not to fall into the temptation of being wise in our own eyes so that we miss his direction for our lives. I find this overwhelmingly encouraging: God is not the author of the negative events of our lives, and if we follow his wisdom, we can avoid many of the potential pitfalls of life.

Sadly, not everyone feels this way about the Word of God.

Recently, a grown man was almost ready to go to blows with me because I said that God doesn't cause or allow negative circumstances for the purpose of instructing his children. He viewed his past failures and hardships as God's instruction, rather than the result of his own and others' free will. It was easier for him to believe that God caused his trials than to acknowledge that his situation was a result of his own choices.

This man failed to see the empowerment that comes from recognizing that our hardships are often a result of our own choices. If we made the choices that caused us to arrive at that place, then through God's wisdom, we can make the choices needed to lead us out. This man's desire to protect his ego by ignoring his own personal responsibility outweighed his ability to grasp the true nature of God. As a result, he—and countless others like him—missed out on the freedom found in realizing that God's desires and intentions toward us are always and completely good.

Furthermore, failing to align our own ideas and opinions to God's is what produces the pain that is experienced in godly discipline. When God speaks and I respond by aligning my thoughts and opinions with his, although it may be painful to my ego in that I must come face-to-face with the fact that I'm wrong and God is right, in the end I rejoice, because his ways lead to life. It is as the writer of Hebrews states, "No discipline seems pleasant at the time, but painful. Later on, however, it produces a harvest of righteousness and peace for those who have been trained by it" (12:11).

God's rebuke toward us, through his Word, is the proof of our sonship. The writer of Hebrews also says, "If you endure chastening [*paideuô*], God deals with you as with sons; for what son is there whom a father does not chasten?" (12:7 NKJV). The NIV translates the first part of verse 7 as, "Endure hardship as discipline," but the word "hardship" is not found in the original text. It was added by translators, I assume, because they thought it would flow better, but unfortunately, their choice sacrificed intent for readability—which in the case of Scripture is never a good idea. The writer is not trying to state that hardship is the proof of our sonship. If that were the case, then the whole world would be saved, for everyone undergoes adversity. Rather, the writer states that *paideuó*—or specifically, *discipline*—from our Father is proof that God claims us as his children. (For further evidence that God's discipline comes through his Word, see 2 Timothy 3:16, where Paul teaches Timothy that the Word of God, not hardship, is "useful for teaching, rebuking, correcting and training in righteousness.")

Our human fathers, the writer tells us, discipline us physically, but our heavenly Father disciplines us spiritually. Sickness and tragedy exist in the physical realm alone; they aren't spiritual tools, and they certainly aren't the methods of a spiritual God. Some might point to Old Testament stories such as Sodom and Gomorrah, the Flood, or the plagues sent against

Egypt; however, these were not instruments of discipline but rather acts of judgment. The intent was the destruction of the evildoer and not the training of God's people.

Words, on the other hand, are spiritual. Through faith-filled words the world was formed, a virgin named Mary was impregnated by God, and our dying Savior uttered the words, "It is finished" to fulfill the Mosaic Law once and for all (John 19:30). Even today, we enjoy the benefit of our salvation now and forever through the confession of our mouth. As Proverbs 18:21 says, "The tongue has the power of life and death, and those who love it will eat its fruit." Words have power. They move mountains and break down walls.

I suppose one reason that so many of us miss God's direction for our lives is because we've become so codependent upon circumstances to shape our path that we have little use for hearing God's voice in our hearts. In our minds, our circumstances provide the final authority. As Solomon says at the introduction to his book of wisdom, "Fools despise wisdom and instruction" (Proverbs 1:7)—in other words, if we rely on the school of hard knocks to teach us, we pay no attention to the words that can change our lives.

Fools receive a rebuke or chastisement as criticism, whereas a wise man sees it as an opportunity to learn something new and to enhance his personal abilities. As Psalm 94:12 says, "Blessed is the one you discipline, LORD, the one you teach from your law." When we understand that God's chastisement is not circumstantial, we see God's discipline the way he meant us to receive it—as an encouragement. Be careful not to confuse discipline and hardship. As we'll see, finding joy in discipline and finding joy in hardship or trials are two totally different mind-sets.

ABRAHAM AND ISAAC

A few years back, I took a tour of a moderate-sized vineyard along the coast of Lake Michigan. From the tying of the young vines to the lines, to the final artistic presentation of a rich glass of merlot at the table, I was struck by the precision and attention that went into every step of the winemaking process. What stood out to me the most was the testing of the wine prior to its bottling. The winemaker uncorked the barrel, filled his glass, and swirled around the small sample. He examined the tannins, the smell, the color, and then finally the taste by slowly swooshing it around in his mouth and slurping it between his cheeks. When he was finished, he had to decide, considering all factors, whether the wine was ready for consumption. It dawned on me that God's testing happens in much the same way.

Consider the story of Abraham and Isaac in Genesis 22. The Lord asked Abraham to take his and Sarah's only son, Isaac, and sacrifice him as a burnt offering on top of a nearby mountain. Early the next day, without telling anyone the purpose of his mission, Abraham gathered his son, enough wood for the burnt offering, and two of his servants and left for the mountains to sacrifice his son as the Lord had commanded. At the end of their journey, as Abraham's only son lay bound on the altar waiting for his father to give the sacrificial cut with the knife, God provided a ram that was caught by its horns in the nearby thicket. Abraham joyously slaughtered the ram, offering it in the place of his son Isaac. And God, in his goodness, provided an acceptable sacrifice (a foreshadowing of the death of Christ, I might add), without allowing Abraham to kill his son.

What would have happened had Abraham decided *not* to sacrifice his son Isaac on the altar? I believe that like the winemaker testing the wine, Abraham's rejection of God's request simply would have revealed to God that Abraham was not yet ready for use. In either scenario, Isaac would have lived, but by refusing to follow God into the unknown, Abraham would have missed out on experiencing God's full intention for his life.

Ironically, Scripture reveals that Abraham already knew that God would provide a way out. In fact, Abraham told his servants in faith that he and Isaac were going to go worship "and then *we* will come back to you" (Genesis 22:5). The Hebrews passage reveals to us that his statement wasn't just wishful thinking on Abraham's part. The passage continues, "Abraham reasoned that God could even raise the dead, and so in a manner of speaking he did receive Isaac back from death" (Hebrews 11:19).

You see, God's "testing" of Abraham was done not to bring harm into his life but to expose his readiness to serve God. Yes,

God asked Abraham to slay his only son, but God never would have let that happen, and Abraham knew it! When Abraham said yes to God, God saw a visible demonstration of Abraham's willingness to follow him no matter what. In his heart and through his actions, Abraham was saying, "I trust in you, God! Your intentions for me are good!"

God's testing will never bring harm into our life. God's testing will only expose our motives and intentions. Ironically, I see this most often in the little things. When the Lord speaks to me and asks me, for example, to invite someone to church or pray for someone in need, I believe what God desires to know in those moments is, *Are you ready and willing to follow me?*

> **God's testing will only expose our motives and intentions.**

Others have experienced this same feeling when prompted to go on a mission trip or take some other step of faith.

At times, perhaps all of us have either missed or ignored God's direction in our lives or rationalized our way out of obedience. When we do, as believers, we don't fall under God's wrath; rather, we simply show God that we aren't ready for what he desires to do next in our lives, which inevitably is always better than what we are experiencing now.

Like the winemaker, God is evaluating us on multiple factors, not to approve us—for we are already approved in Christ—but to see if we are ready and able to follow him anywhere. This is how we discern what is God's testing and what is not. If it brings harm into our life, it's not God. A test where God does not provide the ram is no test at all—that's an attack, and I assure you, God is not the source.

SPIRITUAL TRAINING WHEELS:
NO TEMPTATION BEYOND WHAT WE CAN BEAR

Most Christians believe that God will allow some testing or temptation into their lives, but that at just the right moment, he'll step in and provide a way out if it gets to be too much for them to bear. Christians draw this conclusion from 1 Corinthians 10:13, where Paul writes, "No temptation has overtaken you except what is common to mankind. And God is faithful; he will not let you be tempted beyond what you can bear. But when you are tempted, he will also provide a way out so that you can endure it."

One litmus test I use in discerning whether a doctrine is biblical is to take said doctrine to the extreme. Allow it to play out in its fullest sense and see if it still aligns with what you know about God.

In the case of the above passage, picture this: Imagine it's a nice summer day and you're on a walk with your spouse in the neighborhood. All of the sudden, a van pulls up and two guys wearing ski masks jump out, throw a bag over your head, and toss you in the van and drive off. Next thing you know, you open your eyes and you're in an old, abandoned junkyard. Your arms and legs are bound. You hear two men talking and the sound of old machinery firing up. Looking around, you realize that you're in an automotive compactor. The massive metal plate above you is moving slowly and deliberately toward you. You're moments away from your obliteration. You can smell the oil and the rust on the machine as it inches closer and closer to you. As the plate finally touches you, you inhale with one last breath, trying to make yourself as skinny as possible, and as the plate squeezes down upon you, you prepare for your death.

Just then, from out of view, one of the men yells, "Stop!" and the machine comes to a screeching halt just seconds before you become mashed potatoes. The massive plate lifts off of you to reveal the man who yelled stop and who is now untying you.

"Who are you?" you ask.

"I'm God," he says.

"What's going on?" you stammer. "Aren't you the one who tied me up in the first place? And who is he?" You point to the red man with the pitchfork.

"Oh, that's my pal Lucifer. We were just waiting to see how much you could take, that's all," he explains.

"Uh . . . I don't understand," you reply.

"Yeah, that's what they all say," he adds. "But, honestly, you did great!"

Does this scenario have any basis in reality? It would seem

not. Yet inevitably, Christian tradition claims that somehow God is to blame for our adverse circumstances and that he's in cahoots with the devil to see just how much we can handle. Have we forgotten that James 1:13 tells us not to be deceived because God doesn't have anything to do with temptation or trials?

I believe what Paul is actually teaching through this 1 Corinthians passage is this: whether through the enemy, this fallen world, or our own bad choices, temptations, trials, and tests will inevitably come our way. These things are simply unavoidable. But through our own personal, physical, or spiritual discipline (like reading the Word, prayer, or watching what we eat), we are fully able to overcome some of these temptations *without* a supernatural way out.

In other instances, God sees that if left alone, the temptation, trial, or test will totally overcome us, due to our lack of spiritual maturity. Therefore, when we are struggling due to our immaturity, God grants us supernatural power to escape or overcome the situation through his superabundance of grace. God isn't allowing certain temptations and not allowing others. In fact, God isn't involved with temptation at all. Instead, God is involved with victory and providing a way where there seems to be no way. This means that we don't ever have to embrace our trials, thinking that perhaps God is putting us through them in order to teach us something. God isn't allowing certain things to happen to you for your spiritual training or personal benefit. God loves you and is constantly working on your behalf. Furthermore, even when you are tempted, He is faithful and will always provide a way of safety beyond that temptation.

THE GREATEST TEACHER EVER: CHRIST IN US!

For some reason, the instructive nature of the Spirit of God is being overshadowed today by the vast and misguided overemphasis on suffering and circumstances as our teachers. I can only assume that this arose from the concern that to hand people over to the care and instruction of the Spirit seemed frightful, especially since our own lusts readily act as an internal prism, bending the glorious truth of God to mean whatever we want it to.

John writes in his first letter, "As for you, the anointing you received from him remains in you, and you do not need anyone to teach you. But as his anointing teaches you about all things and as that anointing is real, not counterfeit—just as it has taught you, remain in him" (1 John 2:27). You see, John understood that the indwelling presence of the Spirit of Christ in us exists, among other reasons, to instruct us. Jesus confirms this as well in John 14:26 when he states, "But the Advocate, the Holy Spirit, whom the Father will send in my name, will teach you all things and will remind you of everything I have said to you."

Does this mean that there is no place for discipleship, teachers, or other instructors? No. But what it does mean is that we should ultimately look to the inner guide, Christ in us, to provide the final word regarding how to maneuver through all of life's circumstances, adverse or otherwise. God's desire from the beginning was to be in such intimate fellowship with us that he himself would be our instructor. And for born-again believers, this is now our deepest reality. God is our teacher—and his intentions are good.

CHAPTER SIX

GOD REVEALED

For His Glory

THE SUMMER BEFORE my freshman year of college, a couple of my buddies and I got jobs digging ditches for a telephone company and installing underground phone cables. As the summer faded into fall, I had finally reached my last day on the job, and I anticipated that my counterparts were up to something. As it turned out they had saved a very special work order for me to complete in honor of my last day on the job. Much to my chagrin, my final mission was to bury a telephone cable inside our city's very own nudist resort. That's right—an entire village consisting of an in-ground pool, a few volleyball courts, a couple dozen worn-down trailers, and lots and lots of old, naked people. I'll spare you all the details, but let's just say these happy-go-lucky sexagenarians were very proud to be displaying themselves in all of their "glory" upon our arrival.

Though this illustration is a bit crude, it paints a pretty clear picture of the definition of the word *glory*—the fullness of a person; nothing hidden; the entirety of a person clearly seen. Yet, in many religious circles, the word *glory* has come to simply mean "God's presence," as in "Let's pray so that God's glory will come down." But both in Hebrew and in Greek, the word *glory* has a much richer meaning, namely "beauty; distinction; pride,"[1] or as I once heard it described, the truest nature of an object.

God's glory, therefore, should reveal to us his truest nature, or what makes him distinct among all other gods. Much like the retired hippies at the nudist resort, when we see God in all his glory, nothing should be left to the imagination, and what we experience should leave no question as to who God is, what he is like, and how he operates.

The most popular definition of *glory*, however, used among Christians and non-Christians alike, is more like "God's ability to wield and prove his power at will." Recently I heard a tragic story of a child who was killed in a car accident. The family, in an attempt to understand and make sense of their circumstances, concluded that the death of their child must have been for God's "glory." And not surprisingly, although the family was saddened by the death of their child, they obediently praised God for giving and taking away.

Although suggesting that tragedies bring "glory" to God sounds very spiritual, these claims are nothing more than a lie made up by the devil and propagated by the very people who are supposed to know God better than any other group of people on earth—his church. Whether they know it or not, what Christians are really saying when they attribute suffering to God is that God's glory (his greatest attribute and most clearly seen characteristic) is his *power*. What follows is also the notion that God will use any means necessary (most commonly through the use of his mysterious and divine-willed power) to make himself known to us and to bring "glory" to his name. The prevailing thought is that God has no qualms reminding us that he has the power to do whatever he wants, whenever he wants.

Have we forgotten that God's thoughts and ways (alleged mysteries to most Christians) are made known to us through his ability to offer love and mercy to those who forsake their wicked ways and turn to the Lord (Isaiah 55:7)? Furthermore, what kind of egomaniacal, self-serving, wimpy god needs to constantly prove his power, especially to his own children? Are we to believe that the Christian God constantly needs to unleash his power in order to prove his supremacy, teach us to fear him, and see just how much we can take? Although adhering to these Christian doctrines helps us spiritualize our trials and hardships, it's time that Christians wake up and exonerate the reputation and character of God!

The Bible says that the entire human race was made for God's glory (Isaiah 43:7), and contrary to popular Christian doctrine, that does *not* mean God created us so that he could show us how powerful he is. If that were true, then we would have no choice but to believe that mankind was created merely as a divine experiment! On the contrary, to be created for God's glory means to understand the riches of his inheritance poured out to us (Ephesians 1:17–19) and to recognize as children of God that he has lavished (and continues to lavish) his love upon

us (1 John 3:1). God created you so that you might know and experience his goodness, not to watch you suffer.

The notion that God would do anything to elevate himself at the expense of the children he dearly loves is simply not true.

The notion that God would do anything to elevate himself at the expense of the children he dearly loves is simply not true. We know this in part because the Bible clearly reveals (not only in word, but also through the actions of Jesus on the cross) that God is love

(1 John 4:8). Take this revelation of God as love and combine it with 1 Corinthians 13:4–8 (the most famous passage on love). Every time you see the word "love" in this passage, I've inserted the word "God," for *God* and *love* are synonymous:

[God] is patient, [God] is kind. [God] does not envy, [God] does not boast, [God] is not proud. [God] does not dishonor others, [God] is not self-seeking, [God] is not easily angered, [God] keeps no record of wrongs. [God] does not delight in evil but rejoices with the truth. [God] always protects, always trusts, always hopes, always perseveres. [God] never fails.

In light of this passage, it would be impossible for God to harm us in order to bring attention to his deity, because God *never* seeks to serve himself. Furthermore, the Bible also tells us that God has elevated his Word above his name (Psalm 138:2 KJV). What that means is that faithfulness to his Word and the fulfillment of his promises are of greater consequence to the Lord than his own fame, personal recognition, or self-aggrandizement. Because of his promises of unfailing love, forgiveness, and patience (displayed in the death, burial, and resurrection of Jesus Christ), we can be sure that our God is never the source of our suffering.

LORD, HAVE MERCY!

Heralded as one of the flagship chapters about God's glory, Romans 9 is the source of much of our continued confusion about God's character and goodness. Paul writes in verses 17 and 18 of Romans 9:

> For Scripture says to Pharaoh: "I raised you up for this very purpose, that I might display my power in you and that my name might be proclaimed in all the earth." Therefore God has mercy on whom he wants to have mercy, and he hardens whom he wants to harden.

To one who is familiar with the outcome of Pharaoh's life in the book of Exodus, it's easy to view this passage through a lens of God utilizing the king's destruction to bring attention to God's ability to do whatever he wants, especially in the case of unleashing his judgment on sinful man.

Yet one of the reasons Romans 9 creates so much controversy among believers throughout various denominations is that most fail to investigate the origin of Paul's comments about Pharaoh. The exact context from which Paul writes in Romans 9 is taken from God's words to Pharaoh in Exodus 9:15–17:

> For by now I could have stretched out my hand and struck you and your people with a plague that would have wiped you off the earth. But I have raised you up for this very purpose, that I might show you my power and that my name might be proclaimed in all the earth. You still set yourself against my people and will not let them go.

When read in context, we see that Pharaoh's destruction was not the subject of God's admonishment. Moses informed Pharaoh that God easily could have destroyed him in just one plague, but that God raised Pharaoh up for the intention of showing his power in Pharaoh's life and for him to consequently praise God for his mercy!

This perspective is confirmed through God's great patience with Pharaoh during the span of the ten plagues. Hopeful that Pharaoh would humble himself and follow the Lord's decree through his servant Moses, he gave Pharaoh multiple chances to obey, until ultimately Pharaoh was destroyed for his own lack of judgment and wicked rebellion against the word of the Lord and God's people!

"But, wait a minute!" you might say. "The text clearly states that God hardened Pharaoh's heart!" This is true. God did indeed harden Pharaoh's heart. But think of the interaction between God and Pharaoh through the lens of the following analogy. A friend of mine once shared a story he had heard regarding the "hardening" of Pharaoh's heart.

"Imagine leaving a chocolate bar out in the sun on a hot summer day," he said. "What would happen to it?"

"The chocolate bar would melt," I concluded with my lightning-fast analytical skills.

"Now imagine leaving a grape out in that same sun," he added. "What would happen to it?"

"The grape would eventually turn into a raisin," I replied, feeling notably proud of myself thus far.

"So answer this question," he prompted as he leaned in. "Did the sun melt the chocolate bar?"

"Of course," I said, not sure where this was going.

"So why didn't the sun also melt the grape?"

"Because a grape doesn't melt under the effects of the sun. It turns into a raisin," I said, beginning to see what he was getting at.

"Precisely," he concluded. "Although the sun did in fact melt the chocolate bar, the chocolate bar's consistency is what determined the effect the sun would have on it. In the same way, the makeup of the grape determined that it would turn into a raisin, not melt, under the effects of the same sun. In each instance, the sun is constant. But under the effects of the sun, the chocolate bar will always melt, while the grape will always shrivel. The sun doesn't determine the outcome. The *composition* of each of the items is what determines their reaction to the sun. The same was true of Pharaoh."

Interestingly enough, biblical linguistics supports this theory as well. In the original language, the word used to describe the hardening of one's heart is *châzaq*, which means "to strengthen, prevail, harden, be strong, become strong."[2] As in the example of the chocolate bar and the grape, *châzaq* implies a strengthening of an already existing condition. Contrary to popular tradition, God's actions toward Pharaoh should not be seen as God forcing a specific belief or outcome upon Pharaoh. Rather, God's actions could be said to strengthen Pharaoh's already existing opinion of God.

Pharaoh had multiple opportunities to humble himself and change his opinion, but because Pharaoh's heart was bent on rebellion, his heart became continually hardened with each request to let God's people go. God's actions may have *enhanced* Pharaoh's perspective of God, but they didn't *create* Pharaoh's perspective of God.

GOD'S GLORY AND HIS GOODNESS

For many Christians, the word *glory* tends to promote more mystery about God than revelation about his nature. One time a pastor shared with me, "When I walk into a church, I can tell right away if God is present or not."

"Oh yeah? How's that?" I asked, unsure where this conversation was headed.

"By the glory cloud," he said authoritatively. "When I walk into a church, I look in the auditorium and if I see the glory cloud, then I know it's a kingdom-oriented ministry," he concluded.

As a pastor, it's easy to assume that people must be experiencing the intimate presence of God when we hear of the miraculous happening in someone else's church or we see the size of someone else's ministry. And clearly for this pastor, God's glory was more about divine mystery, signs, and wonders than the personal revelation of God's nature and truest identity now residing in us.

Ironically, the main character in Exodus was not unlike many Christian ministers today. Moses, who led the largest ministry in the world at that time and who had miracle after miracle accompany him and validate his ministry, admitted to God that he did not know who God *really* was (Exodus 33:12–13). Yet so often as Christians we commonly look to a man like Moses and feel jealousy not only toward his relationship with God but also for the miraculous signs and wonders he saw throughout his lifetime.

Although Moses had experienced what Christians today would call the extraordinary "glory" of God, exemplified in his presence and power among the Hebrews, he still cried out to the Lord to know him. In Exodus 33:12–13, Moses states, "You have been telling me, 'Lead these people,' but you have not let me know whom you will send with me. You have said, 'I know you by name and you have found favor with me.' If you are pleased with me, teach me your ways so *I may know you* and continue to find favor with you."

> God's *glory* and His *goodness* are synonymous.

Moses is saying, "God, you know who *I am*, but you haven't fully shown me who *you are*!" This is a powerful and humbling revelation. Moses spoke to God from out of the burning bush, saw God's power work in him to part the waters of the Red Sea, communed with God on Mount Sinai, and received the Ten Commandments. Yet in all this, Moses cried out, "To be honest, I know you're the God of Abraham, Isaac, and Jacob, but I personally don't really know who you are." Moses recognized that being in the presence of God and operating in the supernatural power of God did not necessarily translate into intimate fellowship with God.

Finally, in Moses' desperate pleading to know God better, he demands, "Now show me your glory" (Exodus 33:18). So in Exodus 33:17 and 19, God responds to this most intimate request by proclaiming, "I will do the very thing you have asked, because I am pleased with you and I know you by name. . . . I will cause all my *goodness* to pass in front of you, and I will proclaim my name, the LORD, in your presence."

Moses asked to see God's glory, and the Lord responded by saying, "I will have my *goodness* pass in front of you." Through this passage of Scripture we see with clarity that God's *glory* and His *goodness* are synonymous. Moses had already experienced the power and presence of God, but the question he had was, "What is your truest nature?" God responded clearly and with great compassion by showing Moses his truest nature and deepest reality—his goodness.

FADING VERSUS SURPASSING—THE GLORY OF GOD REVEALED IN THE NEW COVENANT

As someone who majors in preaching the goodness of God, I am often questioned about, and sometimes accused of, ignoring or minimizing the law and the Old Covenant. I figure that since Paul had to address these concerns on numerous occasions throughout his ministry, I must be in good company. And interestingly enough, Paul specifically addresses this concern regarding God's glory in 2 Corinthians 3:7–12:

> Now if the ministry that brought death, which was engraved in letters on stone, came with glory, so that the Israelites could not look steadily at the face of Moses because of its glory, transitory though it was, will not the ministry of the Spirit be even more glorious? If the ministry that brought condemnation was glorious, how much more glorious is the ministry that brings righteousness! For what was glorious has no glory now in comparison with the surpassing glory. And if what was transitory came with glory, how much greater is the glory of that which lasts!
>
> Therefore, since we have such a hope, we are very bold.

Now, as we have already established, God's glory is his goodness, and thus his goodness is his glory. What Paul is pointing out, therefore, is that the law, or the "ministry that brought death," did come with a "goodness," if you will, in that it revealed to us our sinful nature (Romans 3:19; 5:20; Galatians 3:19; 1 Timothy 1:8). This also means that even despite the condemnation that the law produced, it revealed to us godly precepts by which we could conduct our lives in order to experience life (Deuteronomy 30:19). The goodness inherent within the law remained altogether inferior to what Paul calls the "surpassing glory" of the New Covenant now made available to us through Christ!

You might be a good golfer—that is, until you're placed next to Bubba Watson. Or perhaps someone might consider you a good artist—until your work is displayed next to Michelangelo's. In the same way, an item that possesses a degree of glory (goodness), when placed next to something with infinite goodness, is hardly even worth mentioning or comparing.

Such is the case with the Old Covenant and the New Covenant. Although a glory (goodness and mercy) in fact existed within the context of the Old Covenant, the glory revealed therein was limited by our propensity toward sin. The law may have exemplified God's holiness and revealed our need for a Savior, but it was incapable of bringing about our salvation. It's not that we disregard the law; rather, we should completely and fully esteem Christ.

You may be asking at this point, "If the law is not as glorious as the New Covenant realities found in Christ, then why did God even give the law in the first place?" We will explore the answer to that question in the next chapter; however, the short answer is that God needed to change us. As the writer of Hebrews states, "The law is only a shadow of the good things that are coming—not the realities themselves" (10:1). This transformative work that Christ was to perform in us at the cross would once and for all open the door for us to be found righteous before God through faith, something that the Old Covenant could never do.

CHAPTER SEVEN

THE PURPOSE OF THE LAW

Thou Shalt Not

RECENTLY, WHILE ON VACATION, my wife and I visited a large aquarium. We had been to this aquarium several years prior and besides a few new exhibits, not much had changed. But as we strolled through the aquarium that day, I sensed something was different. I recalled on our former trip how nearly every unruly child was giving even the moray eels a jolt by pounding on the aquarium too hard. It was as if they all saw and read the customary "Please don't touch the glass!" signs and immediately started hitting it. Truthfully, I was at least slightly tempted to do the same, especially if it meant getting my coveted selfie with my wife, a shark, and a docent in the background doubling as someone from the glass police.

But on this day, the entire mood of the aquarium was different. As I casually looked around, I saw people leisurely strolling by and observing the marine life, very contentedly, I might add, at a respectful distance *away* from the glass. Then it dawned on me. All around the aquarium, the countless "Do not touch the glass" signs, formerly positioned strategically on the walls about every five feet, had been removed. Of course, not every child was on his best behavior, nor were all parents bringing their A game while deftly moving their children through each exhibit. But on this day, not one person was touching the glass.

As we meandered through the dimly lit halls of the aquarium, I pondered what rules actually do to people. When we pull on to the highway and see the 65 mph speed limit sign, at what speed do we set our cruise control? When a young boy gets the attention of the girl he likes by pulling her hair, and she correspondingly yells, "Stop it!" what will he always do next? And when we tell our toddlers, "Please don't touch the glass, honey," what can we naturally expect as sure as the day is long? If there is a rule, then you can be sure we will probably break it. Rules are the box to our Pandora and the Mentos to our Diet Coke. Like the mythical sirens of the Tyrrhenian Sea, rules beckon us to violate them. Remove the rules, however, and you remove the catalyst that ignites our rebellion.

HOLY GOD, SINFUL MAN

One of the problems that prevents people from realizing that God is not the one causing our pain is that people have not been taught how to divide the covenants (2 Timothy 2:15 KJV). By mixing the Old and New Covenants, a Frankenstein-like theology is pieced together about God that only perpetuates our confusion. In order to separate our understanding of the two covenants, and consequently the true nature of God, we must first understand the law. It's important to remember that God never intended to relate to us primarily through a list of rules and regulations. As we've discussed in previous chapters, we know that when God created humankind, he gave them the freedom to explore this new world with virtually no limitations or restrictions, save one. His loving nature demanded that he give humankind the choice to enter into a relationship with him evidenced by our obedience or to reject him by going our own way. We chose the latter.

Now, because most people assume that the God of the Old Testament is a God of wrath, we have mistakenly viewed the whole of Scripture through the lens of a vengeful, angry God. For example, according to popular tradition, when Adam and Eve sinned, God kicked them out of the Garden because "a holy God cannot stand in the presence of sinful man." However, if you recall, when Adam and Eve sinned, God actually spared them. Although he had full right to wipe them off the face of the earth, he didn't. Then, although Adam and Eve had thrust all of mankind into a spiritual abyss, God *personally* came to the Garden, discovered where they were hiding, talked directly to them about what they had done, and made a sacrifice to atone for their sins (Genesis 3:8–9, 11, 21). Does this sound like a God who cannot be in the presence of sin?

Furthermore, many theologians teach that the reason God forbade Adam and Eve from reentering the Garden after the Fall was because he was judging them. But in actuality, God was trying to protect them. The Bible says that if Adam and Eve had eaten from the tree of life after having eaten from the tree of the knowledge of good and evil, their fate would have been forever sealed—life immortal in their fallen, sinful state (Genesis 3:22). As a result, he removed them from the Garden and placed an angel on duty to guard the path back to the tree of life. This account was never about God's inability to stand among sinners; it was about God's love and mercy for humanity.

And what of Cain, the man who committed the very first murder recorded in Scripture? What was God's attitude and behavior toward him? God approached him personally to discuss the matter and placed a mark on Cain so that no one would harm him (Genesis 4:15). Noah was a drunk and Abraham a liar, yet not only did God not punish them, but each of these individuals prospered in their relationship with God despite their shortcomings. And what about Jesus? Have we forgotten that Jesus, the Son of God, friend of sinners, came down to dwell among us (John 1:14) and eventually take up our sin? How is it, then, that modern Christian tradition has come to the conclusion

> God has always been, and will always be, first and foremost, a God of love.

that God is still punishing people for their sin through negative circumstances?

God has always been, and will always be, first and foremost, a God of love. God is not an immunodeficient hospital patient, susceptible to being tainted by sin. He isn't repulsed by us or disgusted by our sinful nature. On the contrary, God got involved with our sin. He came down to our mess. He became so closely acquainted with mankind's sin that he became it (2 Corinthians 5:21). The notion that God cannot be in the presence of sinful man is not only totally debunked throughout the Old Testament but also is discredited in light of Jesus' emergence into human history.

GRACE BEFORE THE LAW

For thousands of years prior to the law, God related to people just fine without it. Before the law was given to the Hebrews through Moses, God dealt with mankind's spiritual bankruptcy by adding mercy and *not* taking into account man's sins (Romans 5:13). Furthermore, he even left the sins committed by the people prior to the law unpunished (Romans 3:25)! God's attitude toward humankind and his sin demonstrated quite clearly that his nature is to be slow to anger and to abound in mercy (Psalm 103:8; 145:8).

Because of God's soft dealings with people before the law, an interesting conundrum developed. Since the law was yet not present to define acceptable behavior, and since man's sins went largely unpunished by God, mankind eventually developed an opinion that his behavior didn't matter to God. Furthermore, man reasoned that as long as he was better in comparison to his fellow man, he was justified in his actions.

Consider the comparison between Cain and his distant grandson Lamech. After Cain killed his brother Abel (Genesis 4:8), the Lord not only refrained from judging Cain but also put a mark on his head so that no one would harm him. Later Lamech continued his family's tradition of bloodshed by killing a young man who had wounded him (Genesis 4:23). Since at the time the law had not yet been given, and there was no measurement for holiness, Lamech reasoned that if Cain was avenged seven times (and that by God himself), then he personally should be avenged seventy-seven times, since his murder was in self-defense. Lamech must have thought, *After all, if God truly overlooks our sins and gives us the benefit of the doubt, what difference does it make if I kill someone? Cain got away with it, so God must accept me too!* With this mind-set in place, it didn't take long before sin spread like a wildfire across the earth.

As recounted in the story of the Flood, God's first solution to terminate sin was to start all over. But as time would tell, the disease that infected us all at the Fall didn't take long to manifest in humanity once again. Although Adam and Eve at one time knew they were no longer like God, they, like the rest of us, were ignorant of the metamorphosis that had taken place in them and the spiritual depravity that had engulfed them like a plague. If left unresolved, however, this condition would produce an outcome of eternal separation from God. The only cure remained to reveal how unlike God we now were. Therefore, because of our sin, God added the law (Galatians 3:19). Through the law, he exposed our need for a Savior and created a path that would lead us to Christ.

LAW ADDED

As discussed earlier, a strange tension exists between the human race and the law. Give us rules and we are bound to break them. Paul sheds light on this phenomenon in Romans 5. In verse 20 he states, "The law was brought in so that the trespass might increase." What this means is that God gave the law not only to reveal his holy standard but also to expose our sin *and* to make us sin more! Now you may be asking, "Why would God want us to sin more?" Great question. The answer is because God wanted to bring attention to the fact that we needed a Savior.

Remember that to be right with God—that is, to be genuinely like him—we had to be restored to the position in which we found ourselves prior to the Fall. And of course, this reversal could not truly be accomplished by simply changing our outward behavior. We needed to be changed in our inner being—in our spirit, where the infraction originally took place. Try as we might to stop sinning outwardly, we could never, through our own efforts, change our spirit inwardly. This was something only God could do.

This is how the law works. The commandments bring to life our inner depravity and give us a focal point, if you will, for the lust that is inherent within us. The law excites a desire within us to sin. Then, as the Bible reminds us, "after desire has conceived, it gives birth to sin; and sin, when it is full-grown, gives birth to death" (James 1:15). Had it not been for the law, we wouldn't even have known what sin was (Romans 7:7).

Now, some people falsely conclude that the law is bad. But as Paul points out in the book of Romans, the commandment did not *create* our lust; it simply *exposed* that lust and brought it to light. In other words, the law itself is not flawed; we are. The law exposed how messed up we really were. And like a chink in a knight's armor, our intrinsic imperfection weakened the law and created the opportunity for sin's piercing defeat (Romans 7:8).

Since the law is rooted in behavior modification, it can only affect our physical realm through strict consequences that impact our flesh. The law cannot change our spiritual nature; therefore, it is utterly incapable of saving us from our sin. In fact, contrary to what many people think, mankind can never be made righteous by observing the law. Rather, through the law, we simply become more conscious of sin (Romans 3:20). To continue to look to the law as a means to develop our morals, modify our behavior, or help make us "good" people is simply a losing game.

FIG LEAVES—THE NEW FASHION TREND

In an effort to be justified before God, humankind has employed a variety of tactics through the years to turn attention away from his sin. One of those tactics is to try to cover up our sin. As in the case of Adam and Eve, they thought that with a few fig leaves they could physically cover up their spiritual supernova. I believe this sheds some light on Jesus' response to the fig tree in Mark 11.

When Jesus approached the tree, it gave the illusion of bearing fruit, as it was fully leafed; yet it was in fact empty of fruit. The fig tree was only putting up a facade—it had no fruit and nothing to offer. In the same way, Jesus recalled Adam and Eve's similar attempts to appear holy by covering their fruitlessness. So he cursed the spirit of self-righteousness inherent in us all, as represented by the fig tree—"May no one ever eat fruit from you again" (Mark 11:14). Jesus was reminding us how foolish it is to cover ourselves up with the "fig leaves" of personal effort in an attempt to camouflage our spiritual nakedness. God made it clear then (and would again through the sacrifice of Christ) that only through the shedding of blood can there be forgiveness for sin (Hebrews 9:22).

Interestingly, besides trying to cover up our sin, we often try to create even more parameters to prevent ourselves from sinning. This concept is evidenced very clearly throughout the history of the Israelites. What started out as just ten principles[1] eventually ballooned into 613 *mitzvot* (365 positive and 248 negative), and finally ended up with thousands of rules intended to keep a moral fence around God's people to help inhibit their transgressions.[2] The prevailing thought was that if you could fulfill the easier (and less dangerous) man-made laws, then you could successfully steer clear of the more serious (and deadly) Mosaic Law.

Christians are not exempt from this practice either. In the church in which I grew up, our holier-than-thou requisites sounded like this:

1. You have to be baptized to be saved.
2. You can't speak in tongues, and if you do, you are demonized.
3. You have to wear a suit if you are passing the offering tray.
4. You have to confess your sins in order to take Communion.
5. You have to live a holy life for God to bless you.
6. You have to do good deeds in order to make it to heaven.

Of course, each denomination fills in the blanks a bit differently with its own caveats intended to strong-arm people into living moral lives and simultaneously to stop them from going astray. But sadly, most people have become so confused about which rules to follow that if they haven't walked away from faith altogether, then they are most assuredly on their way. For those who are still hanging on to their faith based upon the belief that they are a good person, when tragedy strikes their lives, they are often filled with doubts about God, unsure why bad things could happen to good people. After all, what did they do to deserve it? Sadly, they are still trying to interpret seemingly Old Covenant events in a New Covenant world.

As Christians, we need to let go of our self-righteousness and stop bickering over which rules we need to follow and realize that the more stipulations we place on people to live right, the more likely they will be to stumble. Ever wonder why so many pastors, elders, and leaders fall victim to affairs, scandals, and other personal tragedies? Oftentimes these are the same people who preach extensively (and sometimes even exclusively) about the law. The more rules we try to follow, however, the more it becomes nearly impossible to live a holy life. That's the nature of the law.

> **The more stipulations we place on people to live right, the more likely they will be to stumble.**

STREET PREACHERS AND SORORITY GIRLS

In our day and age, many people view the law more like an à la carte menu than a hard-and-fast standard of holiness. "I'd like kindness toward my neighbor, loving the less fortunate, and patience in the grocery line, please." All the while, the inner voice of our hearts whispers, "How about charity toward your spouse and being on time to work too?" And in order to even the playing field and make us feel better about ourselves, we like to serve up whatever we're having that day to others.

Several years ago, while walking along a local college campus, my wife and I witnessed a street preacher standing at the corner of a busy intersection. From a distance I noticed he had gathered quite a crowd around him, and although I was curious about what he might be saying, we attempted to walk past unscathed. But when he accused my wife and me of being adulterers as we strolled by, I quickly turned around and tuned in to what he was saying.

"You are all fornicators and prostitutes!" he said addressing his growing crowd. Various people in the crowd fired back insults and rebuttals. Yet he was unfazed.

"There is no one righteous—not even one!" he continued. "All who fail to keep the whole law of God are adulterers and liars!"

As I stood and watched him for a few minutes, I was impressed by his zealousness but shocked by his self-righteousness. "Excuse me," I interrupted. "A moment ago you accused me and my wife of being adulterers. I assume it was because we were holding hands?"

"Oh . . . I didn't know that was your wife," he muttered in a way that did not at all feel like an apology. "Well, all have sinned and fallen short," he continued with his same tired routine.

"Are you saying you are righteous, and everyone else around you is a sinner?" I asked as the crowd grew silent. We all eagerly awaited his reply.

"I live by God's holy law," he retorted in complete confidence.

"So you haven't sinned today?" I asked.

He thought for a second before speaking. "No, I haven't."

Just then, in a moment of divine timing, two attractive and scantily clad sorority girls walked by and caught the young preacher's attention. Time stopped as the man fixated his attention on their backsides. By the time he snapped out of it, he turned back to realize that I saw him ogling their behinds.

"Uh . . . what just happened there?" I asked.

"What do you mean?" he said, obviously flustered.

"You just checked out those girls," I said, calling him out. "Don't you know that the Bible teaches that anyone who looks at a woman lustfully is guilty of adultery?" I asked.

I found out that night that nothing ends a sermon quicker than accusing the preacher of lustful thoughts. He knew he had been caught and his homily was over. But for the next twenty minutes, I spoke with sincerity toward the young man, showing the law as a tool to expose our need for salvation instead of as an obligation we must fulfill. I'd love to tell you that I helped change his view of God that night, but I'm not sure I did. But I do know that when a person is entrenched in legalism as much as this guy was, it won't be long before he hits rock bottom.

ADVENTURES IN BABYSITTING

When the law lays bare our weaknesses, our spiritual depravity, and our desperately fallen state, it draws us to the conclusion that we need God. And that's the law's primary intention. The law was not given to provide us with a moral code or spiritual checklist; rather, it was given to lead us to Christ. In Galatians 3:21–25, Paul writes,

Is the law, therefore, opposed to the promises of God? Absolutely not! For if a law had been given that could impart life, then righteousness would certainly have come by the law. But Scripture has locked up everything under the control of sin, so that what was promised, being given through faith in Jesus Christ, might be given to those who believe.

Before the coming of this faith, we were held in custody by the law, locked up until the faith that was to come would be revealed. So the law was our guardian until Christ came that we might be justified by faith. Now that this faith has come, we are no longer under a guardian.

The word "guardian" in the King James Version is translated "schoolmaster." In Greek, the word is *paidagōgos*, which means "a guardian, and guide of boys."[3] *Vine's Expository Dictionary* further adds that the *paidagōgos* "exercised a general supervision over the child and was responsible for his moral and physical well-being."[4] Today we would refer to this person as a babysitter.

As a parent, when you leave your children in the care of another, that person only has authority over your children for as long as you are away. While you are gone, her function is to keep your kids out of trouble and to ensure their safety. But upon your return, you are no longer in need of her services.

The same can be said of the law. As we see in this passage in Galatians, before faith came, we were under the supervision of the law. The law prevented us, or more specifically the nation of Israel, from being corrupted by this world. But when faith was revealed in the person of Jesus Christ, we no longer needed the services of the Mosaic Law. Additionally, now that faith is present, the law is made obsolete. All that now remains is grace through faith.

JESUS—THE FINAL TEACHER OF THE LAW

Amazingly enough, I think people's greatest hang-up with the message of grace centers around Jesus. As Paul writes to the Romans, "They stumbled over the stumbling stone" (9:32). This Jesus guy seems to be really difficult to figure out. One minute he's loving and kind, and the next he's flipping over tables and throwing insults like lightning bolts on those around him. Certainly these instances of Jesus' life and ministry can be confusing until we understand that he was being intentional with every word and action he took. Jesus' purpose was not only to usher in the New Covenant but also to fulfill and complete the righteous requirements of the Old Covenant.

As we look to Jesus' life, therefore, we must keep in mind that his goal was to expose man's need for a Savior. He had to demonstrate the absolute futility in men and women trying to fulfill the righteous requirements of the law on their own. It is with this mission in mind that Christ entered the world and began his ministry. But in order to uncover mankind's self-righteous attempts at justifying ourselves, Jesus needed to reveal how holy the law actually was. Perhaps no place is this better illustrated than the Sermon on the Mount.

Jesus says in Matthew 5:20, "For I tell you that unless your righteousness surpasses that of the Pharisees and the teachers of the law, you will certainly not enter the kingdom of heaven." Remember, the Pharisees and teachers of the law devoted their entire lives to observing the law! If they weren't good enough to earn salvation, then who was? Jesus was exposing that over time, the Pharisees had developed an attitude regarding the law that implied, "Don't commit adultery? No problem. I can follow that."

But then Jesus ups the ante and adds, "I tell you that anyone who looks at a woman lustfully has already committed adultery with her in his heart" (Matthew 5:28). At that, they were stunned! Who, then, could remain righteous? The answer is—no one could. And this was Jesus' intent—to show us that we don't have what it takes to keep the righteous requirements of the law and that we are all in need of a Savior.

Jesus continues by painting murder, divorce, and oaths in the same light—namely, if you commit the sin in your heart, it's the same as committing the sin in deed. In each instance, Jesus elevated the law to its holiest standard, revealing it to be infinitely more stringent than what people previously thought.

To illustrate this further, let's look at the story of the rich young ruler in Mark 10:17–22. The rich young ruler would fit in well at most of our churches. He was well behaved and devoted, and he scrupulously followed the law. He was what most of us would call a "godly person," and society expected that this man would surely go to heaven. But in actuality, this young man epitomized self-righteousness, and Jesus totally called him out on it. Mark writes,

> As Jesus started on his way, a man ran up to him and fell on his knees before him. "Good teacher," he asked, "what must I do to inherit eternal life?"
>
> "Why do you call me good?" Jesus answered. "No one is good—except God alone. You know the commandments: 'You shall not murder, you shall not

commit adultery, you shall not steal, you shall not give false testimony, you shall not defraud, honor your father and mother.'"

"Teacher," he declared, "all these I have kept since I was a boy."

Jesus looked at him and loved him. "One thing you lack," he said. "Go, sell everything you have and give to the poor, and you will have treasure in heaven. Then come, follow me."

At this the man's face fell. He went away sad, because he had great wealth.

Well versed in the Mosaic Law, this man approached Jesus seeking justification—a spiritual pat on the back, if you will—regarding all the ways he had earned his righteousness before God. At this, the Bible says, Jesus loved him and responded, "One thing you lack." Consequently, the man received the exact opposite of what he had hoped. Instead of accolades, Jesus unveiled the full extent of the law and stated, "You're still missing something."

Ironically, I believe that even if this man had sold everything he owned, given it to the poor, and returned to Jesus, Jesus' response to him still would have been the same: "One thing you lack." Why? Because no matter how many good deeds we do, or how good a person we think we are, without Christ, our own righteousness is like filthy rags (Isaiah 64:6). As Romans 3:20 teaches, "No one will be declared righteous in God's sight by the works of the law." Even if it were possible for you to fully observe the law, the law still would remain incapable of pronouncing you righteous. Only faith in Christ can get the job done.

CHAPTER EIGHT

REMOVING THE MIXED GOSPEL

Roller-Coaster Christianity

I USED TO BE a full-blown legalist. Sounds sort of menacing, doesn't it? But I was. Sure, I would have told you that God loved you, but with every acknowledgment I made about God's love, I followed it up with so many other qualifying statements and caveats that the words became totally void of their power. I was the king of, "Yes, but" statements. "*Yes*, God loves you, *but* you also have to obey his Word." "*Yes*, God wants you to be healed, *but* you have to be in his will in order for him to hear your prayers," or "*Yes*, God wants to take care of your needs, *but* you have to stop sinning if you expect him to bless you." In our denomination we walked a fine line between law and grace, and most of us would have probably lobbied for some balance between the two.

The people in my church had enough love to lead people to Christ but enough law to make sure they continued to live holy once they found him. That was sort of our unwritten motto. The theory sounded good on paper and in our doctrinal statement, but our need to balance law and grace was a direct result of our utter discomfort with the extreme nature of God's love. Call it tradition or whatever you want, but somehow we could never seem to let the unconditional love of God sink in.

Toeing the line between law and grace inevitably led me down a path I refer to as "roller-coaster Christianity." When I was at the summit and doing well (i.e., performing according to a predetermined yet arbitrary set of standards) my life seemed to flourish and all seemed right with the world. But whenever I fell short of this fixed standard, I nose-dived into despair by the g-force of whatever mistake I made that day or that week. Inevitably, a feeling of depression, alienation, and separation set in, until I mustered up enough energy to *chink, chink, chink* my way back up to the crest of right standing with God. Locked into a ride from which I could never get off, my only option seemed to be to hang on tight, hoping I'd survive another plummet. Then the never-ending cycle began all over again. Until we are able to exit the roller coaster of performance, we will continue to assume that our negative circumstances are punishment for our sinful behavior.

THE MIXED GOSPEL

Many of the false doctrines about the nature of God, which have been discussed in this book, stem from what is sometimes referred to as "the mixed gospel." Boiled down, the mixed gospel is any attempt to balance law and grace—a little law here and a splash of grace there—with the goal being to offer people enough love and acceptance to get them saved, but then to teach them all the rules they must follow in order to keep their salvation. By mixing the two covenants, religion has created a picture of God much like my neighbor's dog. Most of the time his dog is as friendly as can be, but don't make a wrong move, because he'll bite your hand off as soon as look at you. Some Christians tout that their God is the best one out there, but once you're part of his family, you find out their explanation of him is more like an abusive stepfather. A god like this deserves therapy, not worship, and in my opinion is no god at all. Until we learn how to embrace the gospel in its entirety, we will always call God's nature into question when faced with negative circumstances.

In my experience, fear is usually the main culprit behind most Christians' abandonment of the gospel in favor of a "Jesus *plus* me" message. Afraid that our righteous deeds can no longer achieve for us the favor of God we think we deserve, we look for a way to add to the saving work of Jesus Christ and inadvertently taint the purity of the message of the gospel. But the many proponents of the mixed gospel claim that a balance between law and grace is paramount. Afraid of the ditches of radicalism so often crashed into by many believers, Christians fear that offering grace is equivalent to giving people permission to participate in sinful behavior. In other words, they say, "Grace gives people a license to sin."

What Christians often neglect, however, is that Jesus preached an all-or-nothing message. "No one will be declared right by observing the law." "Unless your righteousness exceeds that of the Pharisees, you cannot enter the kingdom of heaven." "No one can come to the Father except through me." Christianity, in actuality, knows nothing of "balance." Attempts to balance law and grace don't take Jesus' life and ministry into consideration. The writer of Hebrews says that if we want to know what God is like, then all we have to do is look to Jesus because he's the clear picture (Hebrews 1:3). The law was only a shadow of the good things that were coming—not the reality (Hebrews 10:1).

The cross has no room for company, and any attempt at tempering the goodness of God with wrath and justice dilutes the gospel's power. Although under the Old Covenant God may have issued justice and dealt swiftly with sin, he was never *personified* as wrath. Certainly wrath and justice existed for a time, but once Christ received in his body the full punishment for sin, God's wrath was eternally satisfied and the Old Covenant was complete. Conversely, 1 John 4:16 does tell us that God can be defined as *love*.

The Bible tells us in Isaiah 53:11, "After he has suffered, he will see the light of life and be satisfied." According to this passage, God's justice and wrath were eternally satisfied through his

Son. This is why Jesus in his last breath on the cross confidently uttered the words, "It is finished" (John 19:30 NASB). What was finished? The Old Covenant was fulfilled, and the system of God relating to humankind on the basis of performance was finally over.

The law was useful for a time and successfully led the nation of Israel to the coming of Christ, but now that Christ is come, it is time for the entire world to die to the law so that we can live through Christ. Through the death, burial, and resurrection of Jesus, the wrath of God was fulfilled. This is why the angels jubilantly proclaimed at the coming of Christ in Luke 2:14: "Glory to God in the highest heaven, and on earth peace *to* those on whom his favor rests." This verse is not implying peace *between* one another; rather, it speaks of peace from God *toward* humankind. Christ extinguished the fire of God's wrath and satisfied his demand for justice, ushering in a time of peace.

Isaiah 53 has been cited for centuries as a passage that can help us understand the depth of Christ's suffering on the cross. Yet perhaps even more profound is the passage found in Isaiah 54, which reminds Israel (and consequently all those found in Christ) what God's attitude to her will be once the Messiah accomplishes his life's purpose:

> To me this is like the days of Noah,
>> when I swore that the waters of Noah would never
>> again cover the earth.

So now I have sworn not to be angry with you,
    never to rebuke you again.
Though the mountains be shaken
    and the hills be removed,
yet my unfailing love for you will not be shaken
    nor my covenant of peace by removed,"
    says the LORD, who has compassion on you. (Isaiah
    54:9–10)

Amazingly, in the above passage, the Lord reveals that his love for us is like the promise he made to Noah. Unlike the Mosaic covenant, where God's blessings depended upon one's ability to keep the law, Noah's covenant with the Lord was unique in that it was one-sided. God's promise to never again destroy the earth was not contingent upon our ability to keep a promise or to uphold a certain standard of moral excellence.

The Noahic covenant was based upon God's faithfulness— so much so that God states he will never be angry with us again! For centuries, religion has been telling people about the anger and wrath of God, but he himself states that because of the suffering of his Son, his wrath has been satisfied and he will never remove his covenant of peace. As I like to say, "God's not mad *at* you; he's mad *about* you!" Because of Jesus, we have entered into a New Covenant with God through faith, ratified through the blood of Jesus and based upon God's faithfulness, not ours.

For God to continue to punish sin in New Covenant believers after Christ has paid for our sin would be for him to nullify the work of Jesus on the cross. In our modern judicial system, this is referred to as double jeopardy, and it completely violates the principles of justice. Once a crime is committed and paid for, the perpetrator is exonerated once and for all. In this case, we did the crime, but Jesus paid the time. Therefore, when we are found in Christ, we can no longer be punished again.

WHEN GRACE WAS BORN

When it comes to spiritual pedigrees, the lineage of John the Baptist is near the top of the list. His father, Zechariah, belonged to the priestly division of Abijah; and his mother, Elizabeth, was a descendant of Aaron, the first high priest. Both of John's parents found the strength of their bloodline in the stability and tradition of the law. But, despite their faithful obedience and spiritually fruitful family tree, they were barren and growing older by the day.

As Luke's account reveals, one day while Zechariah was serving at the temple, the angel Gabriel appeared to him and said, "Do not be afraid, Zechariah; your prayer has been heard. Your wife Elizabeth will bear you a son, and you are to call him John" (Luke 1:13). Zechariah doubted Gabriel and as a result, the mighty angel left the old man unable to speak until the time of his son's birth. As Zechariah emerged from the temple that day, literally speechless, the Bible says that the people present soon realized that he had seen a vision, "for he kept making signs to them but remained unable to speak" (Luke 1:22). Zechariah remained in this condition until after John was born.

Once the pregnancy reached full term, Elizabeth delivered their miracle baby. As all of their relatives gazed in amazement at the boy, they began discussing what to call him. The consensus seemed to be to name him Zechariah after his father, but Elizabeth abruptly spoke up and said, "No! He is to be called John" (Luke 1:60). At this the relatives became confused, since the custom in Israel was to name the child after a patriarchal member of the family. But in perfect harmony with his wife, Zechariah penned onto a writing tablet, "His name is John" (Luke 1:63). This was John the Baptist's entrance into the world.

Here we see the beauty of biblical typology and symbolism. Zechariah and Elizabeth, both pictures of the law, opened their womb in order to make way and give birth to the grace of God, seen in John. The name John was special, in that it was originally inspired by the Hebrew variation of the word "Yahweh is gracious." Isn't it interesting that God would come to parents so richly vested in the tradition and religious heritage of the law and tell them to name their son "God is gracious"?

Consider the way the Old Covenant law is illustrated through the story of John the Baptist:

THE LAW	ZECHARIAH AND ELIZABETH
The law carried God's secret wisdom, in types and shadows, unable to reveal the fullness of the gospel until the proper time (1 Corinthians 2:7–8; Hebrews 10:1).	Zechariah was silenced because of unbelief and unable to speak the full revelation from Gabriel and forced to rely upon making signs to communicate the truth.
Under the law, our sins are remembered and judgment rendered.	Zechariah's name means, "The Lord remembers."
Our performance and religious calisthenics are not enough to produce life.	The couple was barren, unable to reproduce.
Before faith came, we were "held in custody under the law, locked up until the faith that was to come would be revealed" (Galatians 3:23).	Elizabeth remained "in seclusion" for five months of her pregnancy until she began to show.
The law was engraved on stone tablets.	Zechariah could only speak through writing on a tablet.

The angel Gabriel entrusted this aging couple with the crucial responsibility of bringing forth a child, who was born with a unique purpose: to lead Israel to the person of grace, the coming Messiah. So, too, was the law put in charge of us for a time to lead us to Christ (Galatians 3:24). The life of John the Baptist, whom Jesus refers to as the greatest who had ever been born of women (Mathew 11:11), further elucidates the role of the law in light of the reality of grace.

John, as Isaiah prophesied, would become a forerunner to the Messiah—one who would show the way. He was a powerful teacher and gathered quite the following as he preached and baptized. Once, shortly after John baptized Jesus, some of John's disciples heard that Jesus was now preaching and baptizing others. Loyal to their teacher, John's disciples came to John to warn him, "Rabbi, that man who was with you on the other side of the Jordan—the one you testified about—look, he is baptizing, and everyone is going to him" (John 3:26). Unfazed, John replies, "The bride belongs to the bridegroom. The friend who attends the bridegroom waits and listens for him, and is full of joy when he hears the bridegroom's voice. That joy is mine, and it is now complete. He must become greater; I must become less" (John 3:29–30). Clearly John understood his role.

The role John would play in ushering in the ministry of Christ was also evident in his teaching. Although we don't have much recorded of the content of John's messages, we do know that he often proclaimed, "Repent, for the kingdom of heaven has come near" (Matthew 3:2). With our modern-day religious filter this sounds like one more judgmental statement from another angry preacher. But if this was the case, then what caused so many to flock to the desert to hear this man? I would offer that it was because John was saying something that had never before been proclaimed.

By this time, the Jewish nation had grown accustomed to living far from God. From the days of Moses, when Moses would meet with God on the mountain by himself, to the temple of their day, where a single high priest would enter into the Holy of Holies to fellowship with God, Israel was no stranger to the chasm that existed between holy God and sinful man. But John the Baptist pleaded, "Change your thinking! The kingdom of heaven has come near to us!"

John announced that gone were the days of trying to climb the moral ladder in order to reach God. On the contrary, through Christ, God has come near to us! Prophesying about the forthcoming ministry of John the Baptist, Isaiah states, "Comfort, comfort my people, says your God. Speak tenderly to Jerusalem, and proclaim to her that her hard service has been completed, that her sin has been paid for" (40:1–2). John, born out of the law, came to testify in grace that the law had been fulfilled and that the Messiah had now come!

The story of Zechariah, Elizabeth, and their son, John, reminds us that law and grace aren't in opposition to one another. Rather, the law existed to serve and bring about grace, just as a mother carries and births a child. The law wasn't against grace any more than Zechariah or Elizabeth were hostile toward John.

Instead, the law rejoiced and welcomed grace into the world; for once grace arrived, the law's purpose was complete. In Christ, we no longer have to live in fear of punishment ever again.

ENTERING THE PROMISED LAND AND LEAVING MOSES BEHIND

In the last chapter of the book of Deuteronomy, Moses, facing the end of his life, addressed the children of Israel along with his successor, Joshua.

> Then Moses went out and spoke these words to all Israel: "I am now a hundred and twenty years old and I am no longer able to lead you. The LORD has said to me, 'You shall not cross the Jordan.' The LORD your God himself will cross over ahead of you. He will destroy these nations before you, and you will take possession of their land. Joshua also will cross over ahead of you, as the LORD said. And the LORD will do to them what he did to Sihon and Og, the kings of the Amorites, whom he destroyed along with their land. The LORD will deliver them to you, and you must do to them all that I have commanded you. Be strong and courageous. Do not be afraid or terrified because of them, for the LORD your God goes with you; he will never leave you nor forsake you."
>
> Then Moses summoned Joshua and said to him in the presence of all Israel, "Be strong and courageous,

for you must go with this people into the land that the LORD swore to their ancestors to give them, and you must divide it among them as their inheritance. The LORD himself goes before you and will be with you; he will never leave you nor forsake you. Do not be afraid; do not be discouraged." (Deuteronomy 31:1–8)

After having led Israel for forty years out of slavery in Egypt and during all of their wanderings in the desert to the edge of the Promised Land, Moses himself failed to enter. I can remember reading this story for the first time as a young teenager and being absolutely devastated for Moses. This man, who had worked so hard on behalf of a people who not only never fully appreciated him but put him through utter misery with

> **In Christ, we no longer have to live in fear of punishment ever again.**

their testing, bickering, backbiting and rebellion, was himself kept from the promise! It just didn't seem fair.

But what I didn't understand then was that Moses was the embodiment of the law—so much so that the law was often referred to as the *Mosaic Law*. Therefore, like Moses, the law was only capable of leading us to the edge of the Promised Land. It was totally incapable of leading us into our inheritance. As we discussed in the previous chapter, the law acted as a guardian until faith in Christ could be revealed (Galatians 3:24–25). The law (Moses) was necessary while the promise (Christ) was away, but when the promise (Christ) came, the law (Moses) was not only no longer needed but was actually *forbidden* to cross over to the other side. What this means is that as New Covenant believers, in order to enter into the promised land of abundant relationship with God, we must leave the law behind.

In the same account, God had given Joshua, the successor of Moses, a daunting task—take possession of the Promised Land and usher in the Israelites. In order to accomplish this, however, he was commanded to eliminate the enemies of Israel in order to make a way for them to enter. Yet despite God's instructions not to make agreements with the current inhabitants of the land, in Joshua 9:3–6, we read about men from Gibeon, neighbors to the Promised Land, who concocted a plan to deceive Joshua into making a peace treaty between them and Israel:

> When the people of Gibeon heard what Joshua had done to Jericho and Ai, they resorted to a ruse: They went as a delegation whose donkeys were loaded with worn-out sacks and old wineskins, cracked and mended. They put worn and patched sandals on their feet and wore old clothes. All the bread of their food supply was dry and moldy. Then they went to Joshua in the camp at Gilgal and said to him and the Israelites, "We have come from a distant country; make a treaty with us. . . .

"These wineskins that we filled were new, but see how cracked they are. And our clothes and sandals are worn out by the very long journey."

The Israelites sampled their provisions but did not inquire of the LORD. (Joshua 9:3–6, 13–14)

On this day, Israel was deceived. This account foreshadowed an eerie picture of the deception that would encroach on believers to come. In these last days the church has been approached by neighboring teachers who, too, have tried to con the body of Christ. Just as the Gibeonites boasted of their long journey, these teachers boast that we should listen and adhere to their long traditions. And just as the Gibeonites pleaded with Joshua, so, too, these teachers plead with the church to make a treaty with them. "Accept our teaching!" they beg. But their bread is moldy, their wineskins are cracked and useless, and if we fall for their ruse, like Israel, we, too, will become deceived.

The teaching these imposters so desperately want the church to embrace is this: the church should "balance" law and grace. But Jesus reminds us in Luke chapter 5 to avoid making such treaties with teachers who insist on blending the Old and New Covenants.

No one tears a patch out of a new garment to patch an old one. Otherwise, they will have torn the new garment, and the patch from the new will not match the old. And no one pours new wine into old wineskins. Otherwise, the new wine will burst the skins; the wine will run out and the wineskins will be ruined. No, new wine must be poured into new wineskins. (Luke 5:36–38)

As an agrarian people, Jesus' audience understood the dangers of placing new wine in old wineskins. As wine ferments, it lets off carbon dioxide, which stretches the skin of the leather to its limit. Once a skin is stretched, it cannot be stretched again or used for new wine, because it would burst and both the wine *and* the skin would be ruined.

Jesus used this parable, therefore, to paint a picture of the danger of carrying the New Covenant in the parcel of the Old. When the Old Covenant and New Covenant are mixed, both the new wine (grace) and the old wineskin (the law) are harmed. Grace is stifled by the condemnation and performance associated with the law—and likewise, the law becomes impotent, incapable of leading anyone to Christ.

YOU'RE HOT THEN YOU'RE COLD: THE CHURCH OF LAODICEA

The problem with all of the misconceptions about law and grace is that their source is often found in the Scriptures. If the sources of these rumors were completely made up, these misunderstandings would be easy to dismiss. But because these mixed-gospel narratives originate in the Bible, they further ingrain in our minds that these teachings must be true, thus tightening the chain of wrong thinking around our necks. After all, what good-natured Christian wants to appear to disagree with the Word?

Yet in our pursuit to remove the shackles of mixed teaching, let's take a look at an additional source of confusion found in the book of Revelation. In Revelation 3:15–16, we read that an angel speaks to the church of Laodicea issuing a strong rebuke: "I know your deeds, that you are neither cold nor hot. I wish you were either one or the other! So, because you are lukewarm—neither hot nor cold—I am about to spit you out of my mouth."

If you're unfamiliar with the Scriptures as a whole, then this verse is perhaps one of the scariest passages in the Bible. As a kid, I can remember being in church and hearing the pastor preach on this passage. The words painted such a vivid picture to me of God spewing these lazy, so-called "Christians" out of his mouth, as if he were taking a drink of spoiled milk. Though for the most part I felt like I was a pretty well-behaved kid, I couldn't help but wonder if I might be one of the lukewarm ones. That Sunday I ran out of the service to the bathroom and cried, begging God not to send me to hell.

The traditional interpretation of this verse—that if Christians fall victim to a mediocre Christian life, then they are in danger of eternal damnation and separation from God—makes it clear to me why so many people hide from God. The problem with the traditional reading of this passage, however, is that this interpretation doesn't consider the context.

A few verses prior to this passage, in Revelation 3:1, the angel begins with the exact same phrase when addressing a different church—the church in Sardis. He says, "I know your deeds." The angel then defines further with which deeds he is familiar: "You have a reputation of being alive, but you are dead." What this means is that the angel's words to both Sardis and the church in Laodicea were not about poor behavior, as is commonly thought. Rather, the forewarnings were directed at churches that performed deeds with a righteous exterior but an empty interior. In essence, he is saying, "Your works make you look like you're alive on the outside, but on the inside you're actually dead." The concept of *deeds* being defined as mediocre, poor, or even evil behavior is simply not found.

The issue was not that the believers at these churches were marginal Christians, but that their supposedly Christian deeds were steeped in self-righteousness. They approached God with a mixture of law and grace, thinking that their good behavior could earn them right standing before God, although their hearts were far from him (Isaiah 29:13; Matthew 15:8). Consequently, this is why the angel says, "I wish you were either one or the other!"

This part of the passage always puzzled me. I could understand why God would want Christians hot (aka "on fire for God!"), but in light of my false interpretation of this scripture,

I could never figure out why God would also want some Christians to be cold. It didn't make sense. What the angel is actually saying is, "I wish you would adopt either law or grace, but because you're mixing them both, I can have nothing to do with you. Because living with a mixture of both will never lead you to God."

Walking in the warmth of God's love and grace leads to abundant and eternal life. And ironically, living according to the unyielding, impossible-to-fulfill, stone-cold Mosaic Law would eventually lead one to a Savior. This is why the angel proclaims he would prefer those in the church to be either one or the other!

Unfortunately, when it comes to the law, however, most individuals simply try to bend it in order to justify their life-style and to fit their behavior. And sadly, because people only follow the laws they deem important, the law never produces its desired effect. These people rely on a little bit of law and a little bit of grace, and as a result, they not only fall short of the law, but they fail to wholeheartedly embrace the salvation of our God.

> **Walking in the warmth of God's love and grace leads to abundant and eternal life.**

The angel reveals this mixture further in Revelation 3:17: "You say, 'I am rich; I have acquired wealth and do not need a thing.' But you do not realize that you are wretched, pitiful, poor, blind and naked." The issue in

Laodicea was not mediocrity but self-reliance. As the saying goes, the height of blindness is thinking that you can see. Christ ends his letter to the Laodiceans with a choice. He says, "Here I am! I stand at the door and knock. If anyone hears my voice and opens the door, I will come in and eat with that person, and they with me" (v. 20).

This is the same offer presented to us today. "Here I am!" our God lovingly proclaims. Can we see him? Can we hear him? Will we push past our traditional thinking and our misplaced blame in order to see God for who he is—a God of love? Or will we continue to hold on to doctrines of convenience, upholding our false image of God and refusing to believe that his intentions for our life are good? The choice is ours.

CHAPTER NINE

BETTER THAN WE THINK

The Problem with Grace

A FEW YEARS AGO, while working on a short video addressing grace and the homosexual community, I reached out to the sitting vice president of one of California's largest gay and lesbian organizations. I explained to her my intention of making a video about the gospel's response toward homosexuality and said I was hoping she would help me understand current vernacular regarding the gay community. After she educated me on the politically correct terminology, she inquired about my stance on the subject.

For the next twenty minutes or so, I shared with her about the love of God, the finished work of the cross, the dangers of finding our identity in anything other than Christ, our experience in helping homosexuals find a deeper relationship with God, and the gospel of grace. "I'm not saying I agree," she responded. "But I think you've found a way to share a biblical viewpoint on homosexuality that won't cause people to feel judged or condemned." I never expected to hear that. "Of course, you know that gays won't agree with your assessment," she continued, "but my guess is that most Christians won't either. If you ask me, it sounds a lot like the place Jesus found himself in." Under the circumstances, I don't think I could have asked for a better compliment.

In my experience, most people prefer black-and-white beliefs, crisp edges, and straight answers, but grace doesn't always afford this luxury. The problem with grace is that it's messy. There are no hard-and-fast rules to apply; no lists to check; no *i*'s to dot or *t*'s to cross. That's because grace in its purest form is about a relationship—specifically a relationship with God through the person of Jesus (John 1:17). If ever a person could quantify, calculate, or define relationship with God, Jesus did. But he did it in such a countercultural way that his message just didn't compute.

> **The problem with grace is that it's messy.**

To the Jews Jesus was a heretic, and to the Gentiles he was a common fool. "Yet to all who did receive him, to those who believed in his name, he gave the right to become children of God" (John 1:12). This confusion about grace is exactly what Paul writes about in Romans 9:30–33:

What then shall we say? That the Gentiles, who did not pursue righteousness, have obtained it, a righteousness that is by faith; but the people of Israel, who pursued the law as the way of righteousness, have not attained their goal. Why not? Because they pursued it not by faith but as if it were by works. They stumbled over the stumbling stone. As it is written:

> "See, I lay in Zion a stone that causes people
>   to stumble
>   and a rock that makes them fall,
>   and the one who believes in him will never
>   be put to shame."

God chose a radical message and delivered it in an unsuspecting package to an undeserving group of people—the Gentiles. And the interesting thing is that they were desperate enough to accept it.

In context, the stumbling stone Paul is referring to in this passage isn't just Christ—more accurately, it's Christ's *righteousness*. Yet Paul says that this message (that people could be in good standing before God only by accepting Christ's righteousness) was so loud, so large, and so difficult to miss that one couldn't help but stumble over it. The problem was although the Jews heard and saw the message loud and clear, they could not receive it, because it did not fit within their religious paradigm. They were so blindly entrenched in the traditions of the law that a veil covered their hearts and their minds were made dull (2 Corinthians 3:14–15). The sad truth is that even today many fail to experience the goodness and grace of God because they cannot humbly accept Christ's message or the free gift of righteousness. Remember, "if God is for us, who can be against us?" (Romans 8:31).

GRACE TEACHES

Embracing the person of grace does require us to temporarily overlook people's shortcomings, but we do so in order to give the Holy Spirit time to work in people's lives. In our church, people have used profanity while sharing their testimonies, shouted out questions in the middle of our services, or come to church in immodest clothing. But Paul encourages us all to continue in Christ the same way we came to him (Colossians 2:6). The last time I checked, we all came to Christ when we were without God and without a hope in the world.

Traditionally minded people are usually afraid of the gospel of grace for fear that people will begin abusing their freedom. A few years back I was asked to teach at a regional Christian conference with members of multiple denominational churches in attendance. About twenty minutes before I spoke, the organizer of the event asked me what I was going to teach on, and I began to share with him about the grace of God. What ensued completely caught me off guard as he declared, "You can't teach that! If my people heard that they might think they can live however they want and God will still love them!" For him (and many others, I might add), the risk of someone abusing God's love had caused him to completely discount the power of it.

But some people don't realize that God's kindness leads us to repentance (Romans 2:4), and that God's grace teaches us to say no to ungodly temptations, *not* to indulge in them (Titus 2:11–12). After we come face-to-face with the grace of our Lord Jesus and gain the revelation that nothing can separate us from the love of God, why would we ever desire to abuse this love and run after other lovers? Those who think that teaching radical grace will give people a license to sin are not very well acquainted with God's grace. That's because believing in grace and trusting in grace are two entirely different things.

Having a concept of God's grace will cause people to push the limits of freedom, rationalizing that because God loves them unconditionally, it doesn't matter what they do. On the contrary, having a revelation of grace causes people to understand that because they've been transformed into new-creation beings, they are consequently set free from the control of sin (2 Corinthians 5:16–17; Romans 6:6). Those who have a revelation of the true gospel live their lives wholeheartedly trusting in grace. As a result, they limit their freedom in order to give life to those around them. In contrast, those with a limited understanding of grace have not renewed their minds to the new creation reality, and as a result they try to achieve holiness through obedience to the law or through strict personal depravation.

The truth is, for the believer, it should be more natural for us to live holy than to sin. Our new nature is one of holiness. Those who dogmatically hold to the concept that only strict adherence to God's rules will produce holiness ignore the beauty of the new birth and assume that our behavioral propensity as new creation beings continues to be opposed to the work of Christ.

I could walk into any church in America, teach hellfire and brimstone, and motivate people to behave for fear of the consequences. But the type of religious performance produced by this method is superficial at best. When no one is watching, fear is not a strong enough motivator to perpetuate good behavior. Grace may take longer to produce results (remember, grace is based upon relationship and relationship takes time), but in the end grace will yield true godliness.

LAW IS GOOD IF USED APPROPRIATELY

For those of you still having a difficult time embracing the doctrine of grace, I want to clarify and state that it isn't that the law has no application for today; it's only that it isn't for the believer.

Paul makes it quite clear that the law is good when it's used appropriately (1 Timothy 1:8). He writes to Timothy to describe the circumstances under which the law proves useful:

The law is made not for the righteous but for lawbreakers and rebels, the ungodly and sinful, the unholy and irreligious, for those who kill their fathers or mothers, for murderers, for the sexually immoral, for those practicing homosexuality, for slave traders and liars and perjurers—and for whatever else is contrary to the sound doctrine that conforms to the gospel concerning the glory of the blessed God, which he entrusted to me. (1 Timothy 1:9–11)

Paul is reminding Timothy that those who have found their righteousness in Christ no longer have a need for the law. But for those who either claim that they are righteous in and of themselves, or for those who believe that truth is relative, the law can be used to fence people in, exposing their depravity and shortcomings in hopes of leading them to salvation through Christ.

Paul also warns Timothy about people who define their ministry by being teachers of the law. He says they have wandered away from the love of God to pursue "meaningless talk" and "do not know what they are talking about or what they so confidently affirm" (vv. 6–7). Therefore, as ministers of the New

Covenant, we must realize that the law is not the gospel and that our mission is to proclaim reconciliation, not condemnation.

HYPER-GRACE

For many years the church lost sight of the gospel of God's grace and began preaching a gospel of works, legalism, manipulation, and fear. Spiritual maturity was measured by how often we fasted, how much we tithed, or how long we prayed. A friend of mine even told a story of a pastor who would coerce members of his congregation into paying interest on the tithes not given on the Sundays when his people missed church! It's no wonder there's been such a resurgence in the message of grace in recent years.

But some, in an attempt to overcompensate for the judgmental and hate-filled teaching that has proceeded from the pulpits for so many years, have begun proclaiming a "God is so good everyone is saved!" message. In fact, recently some teachers have even been promoting a message that Satan will one day be redeemed.[1] Not only does this idea violate our understanding of love, but it also contradicts Scripture. Because of such extreme and unbiblical teachings associated with grace, critics have negatively dubbed this message "hyper-grace."

Paul warns that, inevitably, extreme messages will rise and fall. In Galatians 1, he writes, "I am astonished that you are so quickly deserting the one who called you to live in the grace of Christ and are turning to a different gospel—which is really no gospel at all. Evidently some people are throwing you into confusion and are trying to pervert the gospel of Christ" (vv. 6–7). Such imposters peddle a message that carries a nuance of truth but perverts the gospel by building upon a false understanding and poor interpretation of Scripture.

While it's true that God doesn't allow bad things to happen, he does allow us to allow bad things to happen. And as justice would have it, hell is a real place. Initially reserved for Satan and his demons, hell will make its debut at the final judgment. The final judgment, however, will not be against those who have sinned, because judgment against sin was issued to Christ on behalf of the whole world over two thousand years ago. The final judgment will simply verify which people have been found in Christ. No one will go to hell for his or her sins. However, millions of people will go to hell because they have not accepted the payment for their sins.

Ironically, the reality of the existence of hell actually gives evidence to the goodness of God. Because of the impending doom of hell, God waits patiently for the world to come to a saving knowledge of him before ushering in the final judgment (2 Peter 3:9). If hell did not exist, God would have no reason to sustain life on this earth as we know it. And since he's a good God, he would have immediately saved humankind from the evil atrocities of this world and rescued his people once Christ was resurrected. If hell is not real, then God is much worse than we thought.

SALVATION MADE EASY

The human race possesses an uncanny ability to complicate our existence, and with that, salvation (Ecclesiastes 7:29). Through traditional doctrines and quixotic expectations, Christians have made it nearly impossible for people to come to Christ. Even our hoops have hoops that people must jump through in order be in relationship with God. But I'm convinced that this isn't God's heart or his plan. I believe salvation should be easy, and exceptionally so.

In one of the most highly debated passages in Christian history, Paul outlines the concept of "salvation made easy" in Romans 8. Paul writes, "For those God foreknew he also predestined to be conformed to the image of his Son, that he might be the firstborn among many brothers and sisters. And those he predestined, he also called; those he called, he also justified; those he justified, he also glorified" (vv. 29–30).

Now, if you want to have a little fun, go to a pastors' conference, say the word *predestined,* and see what happens! But what theologians often forget is that these terms written in Paul's language in a beloved letter to the church at Rome did not always carry with them such hefty theological weight.

When Paul wrote that humankind is "predestined," I believe all he meant was formed with a purpose. The same simplicity can be used for the words *foreknew, called, justified,* and *glorified.* Although I'm certain the following interpretation will lack the complexity to satisfy the great religious thinkers out there, consider this same passage again with the following laymen's definitions inserted into the text replacing the "theological" terms listed above:

> For those God *thought about ahead of time* he also *formed with a purpose* to be conformed to the image of his Son, that he might be the firstborn among many brothers and sisters. And to those whom he *formed with a purpose,* he also *communicated that purpose to them*; to those to whom he *communicated their purpose*, he also *fulfilled* this purpose for them through Christ; and to those for whom he *fulfilled* this purpose [in Christ]; he also *honored* them both now and forever. (Romans 8:29–30; author's paraphrase)

What this passage is really stating is that God is so good he spent an eternity past thinking about us—all of us. Then, because of his goodness, he created us with a purpose, which was to become like Christ.

Yet his master plan didn't end there. God then proceeded to reveal to us (through the law and the prophets) what his purpose was for us—to be included in Christ. He made this clearly known to all of humanity through the Word of God and the testimony of creation, "so that people are without excuse" (Romans 1:20).

But it gets better still. Not only did God think of us ahead of time, create us with a purpose, and tell us what that purpose was, but he also fulfilled that purpose for us through Christ! And all those who embrace this gift of life will be glorified by God both now and forevermore. At the end of his exposé, Paul responds to such great news with this profound declaration:

> What, then, shall we say in response to these things? If God is for us, who can be against us? He who did not spare his own Son, but gave him up for us all— how will he not also, along with him, graciously give us all things? Who will bring any charge against those whom God has chosen? It is God who justifies. Who then is the one who condemns? No one. Christ Jesus who died—more than that, who was raised to life—is at the right hand of God and is also interceding for us. Who shall separate us from the love of Christ? (Romans 8:31–35)

As Paul points out, realizing how much God has done for us should render us mute. We should have nothing left to say. As my good friend and mentor Jerry Grieser once told me, "A love like this will never elicit the response, 'How far can I go and get away with it?'"[2] A true revelation of the gospel of God's love and grace will only make you fall all the more in love with God.

GOOD AND ABLE

Early in Jesus' ministry, a man with an advanced case of leprosy came to Jesus and directed a poignant statement toward the rabbi. "Lord," he said, "if you are willing, you can make me clean." Without so much as flinching, Jesus responded, "I am willing. Be clean!" (Matthew 8:2–3). Like many of us, the leprous man had little doubt about God's ability. He knew if Jesus was God, then he had the ability to heal. What the man did not know, however, was whether Jesus *wanted* to heal him. How surprised and relieved the man must have been when he heard Jesus reply, "I am willing. Be clean!"

Mark's account tells us that immediately upon hearing his words, the leprosy left the man and he was cured (Mark 1:42). Simply realizing that Christ was *willing* was enough to activate the man's faith and cause him to receive the promise. The same is true for us today. Not only is God *able* to right all our wrongs, mend our broken hearts, bind up our wounds, heal our bodies, deliver us from evil circumstances, and set us on a path of knowing him—but he *wants* to!

In fact, not one time did Jesus ever deny anyone the opportunity to be well, prospered, made whole, or healed. Jesus had compassion on the multitudes, and whenever they placed a demand on his desire and ability to help, Jesus heeded the call. The only time Jesus was ever limited in his ability to help people was when they did not believe that he could (Matthew 13:58;

Mark 6:5). Like the leprous man, we must recognize that Jesus is not only able to meet the demands of our everyday human struggles, but he is also willing to do so.

I believe that the absence of God's power in the lives of many believers today boils down to a lack of knowledge regarding the true heart of God. According to the apostle Peter, the knowledge of God's goodness is the key to experiencing his power. Peter offers in his second epistle, "His divine power has given us everything we need for a godly life through our knowledge of him who called us by his own glory and goodness" (2 Peter 1:3). In the original language, however, this knowledge does not simply refer to intellectual knowledge but rather an intimate, experiential knowledge. "Truth is never known until it is experienced," writes Dr. Jim Richards concerning Jesus' words in John 8:32. "When Jesus said, 'Then you will know the truth, and the truth will set you free,' that word for 'know' is an experiential knowledge, not an academic definition. Information cannot set anyone free. But truth experienced is freedom!"[3]

In the gospel, we are introduced to a God who loves us completely—so much so that he sent his Son to prove his love. God was both willing and able to bring about a miracle that would forever change the course of humanity. Christ was willing and able to qualify us to receive the fullness of the promise, and because of his willingness to go to the cross he was able to wipe away all of our sin.

But when we preach a message that calls into question God's

love and power, our teachings become in essence "anti-Christ," meaning that the message is in direct opposition to what Jesus Christ came to accomplish. Jesus didn't just possess God's love and ability. He *was* God's love and ability in the flesh, and he did nothing that he did not first see the Father doing (John 5:19). When we try to buffer God's willingness and ability by holding on to man-made regulations, we nullify the grace of God and cause it to have no effect in our lives (Mark 7:13; Galatians 2:21).

HOPE DOES NOT DISAPPOINT

I'll never forget the first time I rode a train. My family and I were going to take the South Shore Line from South Bend to downtown Chicago. My experience with trains up to that point was mostly through watching old James Bond movies, so I could just picture the adventure—a two-and-a-half-hour European train ride across the country in our own private compartment, with a separate dining car where we could drink wine and eat caviar. *This is the life!* Unfortunately, I didn't realize that the South Shore Line was a *commuter* train. In other

> When we try to buffer God's willingness and ability by holding on to man-made regulations, we nullify the grace of God and cause it to have no effect.

words, it was more like a school bus on a track. It had a bathroom but no private quarters. No dining car. And, as I recall, no
toilet paper in the bathroom. My James Bond fantasy quickly
turned into what felt like a sixth-grade field trip gone wrong.

In the case of my experience on the South Shore, my imagination had been greater than reality. But when it comes to our
imagination about God, we can never outthink his goodness. In
fact, our wildest attempts to classify and contextualize his goodness could never measure up to the reality of how good God
actually is. Can you imagine standing before the Lord on the
last day and having him say, "I appreciate all those nice things
you said about me on earth, but to be truthful, you overshot
me. I'm really not as good as you thought I was." Sounds ab-
surd, doesn't it? That's because the Bible tells us that God's plan
and good intentions for his children are *beyond* the scope of our
imagination (1 Corinthians 2:9). In other words, it's impossible
for us to outthink God's goodness!

I certainly didn't grow up with this perspective, however.
Having been exposed to sermon upon sermon of "Repent!" I
was petrified of eternity and afraid of falling short of God's righteous standard. I didn't want to go to hell, but I sure didn't want
to spend eternity in heaven either. In my mind, Disney World
seemed like a much better final destination than heaven, and
I hoped that with a little bit of coercion, God might see it my
way. But the more I began to understand God's goodness, the
more I realized that the Magic Kingdom had nothing on God's

kingdom, and if I could trust him with my now, I could also trust him with my forever.

A friend once confessed to me, "I want someone to pray for me for healing, but I'm afraid of getting my hopes up."

"Why?" I asked. "Has the earth stopped spinning? Has the sun stopped shining? Have the oceans dried up?"

"No," she answered, obviously confused.

"Then get your hopes up, because the Bible teaches that hope does not disappoint!" (Romans 5:5).

While not getting our hopes up may be good advice when it comes to our stance on earthly relationships, it is horrendous advice when it comes to God. Since we know that God is not the source of our problems, and that he is not causing or even allowing individual trials into our lives, then we can know with confidence that God's will for us is good! I say, "Get your hopes up," because God is faithful. In fact, read what Paul tells Timothy about the extent of God's faithfulness: "If we died with him, we will also live with him; if we endure, we will also reign with him. If we disown him, he will also disown us; *if we are faithless, he remains faithful,* for he cannot disown himself" (2 Timothy 2:11–13).

As you read through the above passage, you might expect Paul to write, "If we are faithless, he will be faithless toward us," but he doesn't. Instead, we learn that even when we falter, God remains faithful. Why? Because, according to Paul, it is impossible for God to disown himself. This is why as Christians we can get our hopes up—because when we are married to Christ, our reality is now perfectly and permanently fixed to his.

FINDING OUR WAY HOME

The path is not the mountain.[4] Few words have impacted me more than this simple Chinese proverb. Too often we find ourselves setting up camp along the journey of life, not realizing that we haven't yet reached the summit of our final destination. In our present day, deconstructionist theology (a system of theology geared toward questioning modern assumptions) has gained significant popularity, and there are no shortages of teachers who will tell you what's wrong with the system, the church, our beliefs, and our thinking. Some are even bold enough to tell you what's wrong with God.

To be honest, I believe that religiosity has swept through the masses in such a way that the deconstruction of our former thinking has become in part a necessity. Much of this book has been focused on demolishing the false notions we have held about God's nature, character, and attributes. Jesus also taught the need for deconstruction, saying, "I am able to destroy the temple of God" (Matthew 26:61). But the difference between Jesus' words and those of many of today's teachers is that he didn't just destroy the temple, leaving it in ruins, but he took the time to rebuild it.

The greatest sign of humility is the ability to change our thinking when truth greater than our own is presented to us.

When I first encountered God's goodness, I was faced with a decision: I could choose to continue in my old mind-set, with my naive opinions and self-justifying beliefs; or I could choose to let go, to stop blaming God, and to enter into a new relationship with him based upon his consistent character and good intentions toward me. It seems like an easy choice, but sadly, even some reading this book will refuse to let go of their former opinion of God for fear of facing their own personal responsibility regarding the outcome of their lives.

Others have spent years blaming God for the pain, hardship, and circumstances they have experienced throughout the course of their lives. Some may have chosen to embrace the pain and trials, seeing every event as God's divine choosing. But my hope is that this book, and the scriptures contained within it, have presented you with another option—a new path.

Already I see evidence that the message contained within this book is stirring up a movement among believers all over the world to rethink how we've viewed God—how our false beliefs have incriminated him, justified ourselves, and robbed the world of the much-needed pure, unadulterated message of God's good intentions and unconditional love toward humankind. I pray that those who see God as he truly is would utilize their revelation for the sake of loving others and leading people to him, resisting the urge to simply win arguments and force their opinions on those around them.

If you read this book and think that the purpose was to

point out all the flaws with religious thinking and others' theology, then unfortunately you've missed the point. Deconstructing our former mind-sets may be a necessary part of the journey, but the destination is not found in destroying past paradigms, but rather in growing in intimacy and fellowship with our Father. The summit is not just knowing about God, or being able to defend him to others, but ultimately it is to have and maintain a real, life-giving relationship with our good God.

A FINAL WORD

THE GOOD NEWS IS we aren't destined to live our lives atop the rocky waves of human imperfection. We can exit the ride of personal effort at any time simply by embracing the unconditional love of God. When I finally realized this, I once and for all got off the roller-coaster ride called religion, and my life has never been the same. Now, more than a decade later, I can honestly say that the goodness of God has totally changed my life.

No longer am I held in bondage to my performance, which, like everyone else's, still varies at times. Nor do I ever wonder what God thinks about me or how he feels toward me, because I know deeply and intimately that nothing can ever separate me from his love (Romans 8:39). I also never feel a need to use my works in order to gain his approval, but instead I work because I am already approved.

Although at one time I thought God's unconditional love sounded too good to be true, I now realize that my understanding of God's goodness, albeit still limited, is only the beginning of my future in Christ. Each day is a journey into realizing the beauty and wonder of a God whose goodness far surpasses anything that I could have ever imagined.

If you're ready to begin a loving relationship with Jesus, then follow these steps to find freedom from your former opinions of God, and begin the journey of seeing God as he truly is.

- Resolve to stop blaming God for any negative circumstances in your life.
- Take ownership of the part you've played in creating your current reality.
- Acknowledge to the Lord situations from your past in which you have judged his motives, viewed him as a co-conspirator in your hardships, or held him responsible for your pain.
- Receive the Lord's unconditional grace and forgiveness for your life. Thank him for not using circumstances to punish you and for always desiring the best for your life.
- Refuse to accept the reasons others (like Job's friends) give regarding why certain circumstances happen in your life—especially the reasons that don't line up with the character and nature of God.
- Share this message with your friends, buy them a copy of this book, and encourage them to begin to see God differently.

ACKNOWLEDGMENTS

Jerry G.—The deal still stands: when I make that first million, I am going to buy you a Hummer.

Dr. Jim Richards—For answering my questions over the years. You paved the way for so many of us.

Andrew Wommack—Your teaching and example have been more than life changing. Thank you for personally sharing your heart and vision with us!

Dr. Tim Storey—Thanks for taking a chance on an Indiana boy and seeing something in me worth investing in. Your friendship and contribution in our lives over the last couple of years has been massively transformative!

Dave Duell—You know this good God better than all of us now. You are greatly missed!

Josh and Hannah—You are the best siblings around. Thanks for believing in me more than I believe in myself.

Mom and Dad—You are two of the most inspiring writers I know. Thanks for sharing with me your creativity and your love for the Lord.

Charlotte Grace—I miss you.

Kassie—Thanks for believing in me. I'm so proud of you.

Jo and Kerry—Thanks for asking so many questions! I tried to answer every one of them in this book. Thanks for always making me find time to laugh throughout the journey.

Bryan and Tammy—You've kept me going more times than you'll ever know. And Tammy, so glad we met in biology class in high school.

Everyone at Oasis Granger—For giving me a place to share my heart week after week. I can never thank you enough.

Everyone in Northwest Ohio—Thanks for letting me birth these ideas within your community!

Matt I.—Thanks for your friendship and sharing your industry knowledge along the way.

The Oasis Staff—Man, you guys have put up with so much helping me see this book become a reality. I am eternally thankful for each one of you!

The Grace Community Worldwide—I love all of you. Let the Gospel Revolution begin!

Oscar—Order a pizza, and I'll be right over.

Kara, Sheena, and Brian—Thanks for juggling the rest of my life while I finished the book.

Becky G.—You've been there since the beginning. Thanks for not giving up on us!

Andrew J.—Thanks for giving me a hand with the original languages.

Everyone at J-House and PCCH—You shaped my perspective of God in very formative years. Thank you!

Jeff G.—Thanks for your mentorship so many years ago. I'm here because of you!

MilesHerndon—You guys are amazing and I owe much of my success to your fantastic creativity and endless support: https://milesherndon.com/.

Bob Dylan—We've never officially met, but after cycling through song after song of yours on my iTunes while writing in local coffee shops, I just felt like I should say thanks.

Brad O.—This is all your fault. Thank you!

Jim C.—We did it. Thanks for catching the vision for this book and cheering me on along the way.

Megan M.—Thank you for being able to keep up with every crazy idea that is in my head!

Everyone at Worthy Publishing—I've been praying for a long time for someone to believe in me and understand the message of this book. Thank you!

Krissy Miles—This book never would have happened without you. My work is infinitely better because of your feedback, edits, and patience. Thanks for listening to all of my necessary ramblings over the years. I'm looking forward to this new phase of our lives. I love you!

NOTES

Chapter 1: Inventing God
1. C. S. Lewis, *Mere Christianity* (New York: Macmillan, 1958), 5.

Chapter 2: God Is Not a Criminal
1. Martin Luther King Jr., *Stride Toward Freedom* (New York: Harper and Brothers, 1958), 51.
2. David Hume, *Dialogues Concerning Natural Religion* (1779). Full text available at http://www.gutenberg.org/files/4583/4583-h/4583-h.htm.

Chapter 3: Sovereign God or Control Freak?
1. John Piper, "Fierce Tornadoes and the Finger of God," Desiring God, March 5, 2012, http://www.desiringgod.org/articles/fierce-tornadoes-and-the-fingers-of-god.
2. Notes on Matthew 14:22, 24 in John Calvin, *Commentary on Matthew, Mark, Luke*, vol. 2, CCEL Edition v1.0 (Grand Rapids, MI: Christian Classics Ethereal Library, 1999), http://www.ccel.org/ccel/calvin/comment3/comm_vol32/htm/xliv.htm.
3. Andrew Wommack, "Sovereignty of God," Andrew Wommack Ministries, accessed September 24, 2015, http://www.awmi.net/reading/teaching-articles/sovereignty_god/.
4. W. E. Vine, *Vine's Complete Expository Dictionary of Old and New Testament Words* (Nashville: Thomas Nelson, 1996), s.v. "sovereign."
5. Dictionary.com, s.v. "sovereign," accessed September 24, 2015, http://dictionary.reference.com/browse/sovereign.
6. J. F. Haught, *God after Darwin: A Theology of Evolution* (Boulder, CO: Westview Press, 2000).
7. Bernard Haisch, *The God Theory: Universes, Zero-Point Fields, and What's behind It All* (San Francisco: Weiser Books, 2006), 43.
8. Alexander Pope, "Essay on Man," epistle 1, A Blupete Poetry Pick, accessed September 24, 2015, http://www.blupete.com/Literature/Poetry/PopeMan.htm.
9. F. F. Bosworth, *Christ the Healer*, 2nd ed. (Grand Rapids: Fleming H Revell, 2002), 67.

Chapter 4: The Man behind the Curtain
1. C. H. Spurgeon, "Satan Considering the Saints," sermon no. 623, delivered April 9, 1865, Metropolitan Tabernacle, Newington, England, http://www.spurgeon.org/sermons/0623.htm; emphasis added.
2. Charles Pierre Baudelaire, "The Generous Gambler," last updated September 2006, http://www.gutenberg.net.au/ebooks06/0607031h.html.

3. Matthew Henry, *Concise Commentary on the Whole Bible* (Nashville: Thomas Nelson, 1997), 415.

4. This phrase is made up of two Hebrew words: *suwm*, meaning "set," and *leb*, meaning "heart." See Vine, *Vine's Complete Expository Dictionary*, s.v. "considered."

Chapter 5: Wisdom and Foolishness

1. John Piper, *Don't Waste Your Cancer* (Wheaton, IL: Crossway, 2011), 6–7; emphasis added.

2. Vine, *Vine's Complete Expository Dictionary*, s.v. "conceited."

3. Billy Graham, "Answers," Billy Graham Evangelistic Association, January 23, 2009, http://billygraham.org/answer/does-god-sometimes-test-our-faith-by-letting-hard-times -happen-to-us-if-so-why-does-he-do-it-doesnt-he-already-know-whether-or-not-our -faith-is-genuine/.

4. The Christian community is indebted to the work and service of Reverend Graham. By disagreeing with his interpretation of this single passage, the author is in no way negating his broader work as an evangelist in our generation.

5. The only variation in the Greek would be found when the word is used in verb form, in which case it would be *peirazó*.

6. Colleen Ferreira, "South Bend Police Say Abuse Leading to Boy's Death among the Worst They've Ever Seen," WSBT.com, November 4, 2011, http://articles.wsbt .com/2011-11-04/duct-tape_30362104.

7. Ibid.

8. Bibleapps.com by Biblos, s.v. "*paideuó,*" http://bibleapps.com/greek/3811.htm.

Chapter 6: God Revealed

1. Vine, *Vine's Complete Expository Dictionary*, s.v. "glory."

2. "The KJV Old Testament Hebrew Lexicon," BibleStudyTools.com, s.v. "*chazaq*," http://www.biblestudytools.com/lexicons/hebrew/kjv/chazaq.html.

Chapter 7: The Purpose of the Law

1. Also known as the Ten Commandments, which, ironically, the Israelites promised they would follow (Exodus 19:8).

2. Mendy Hecht, "The 613 Commandments," Chabad.org (content provided by AskMoses .com), http://www.chabad.org/library/article_cdo/aid/756399/jewish/The-613 -Commandments.htm.

3. "The NAS New Testament Greek Lexicon," BibleStudyTools.com, s.v. "*paidagōgos*," http://www.biblestudytools.com/lexicons/greek/nas/paidagogos.html.

4. Vine, *Vine's Complete Expository Dictionary*, s.v. "guardian."

Chapter 9: Better Than We Think

1. The modern proponents of the devil's redemption often cite obscure quotes from an early church father named Origen. And although Origen seemed to believe that Satan could hypothetically be saved because he possessed free will, he went on to imply that it would

never happen, due to the devil's heart being fixed on rebellion. Origen states in *First Principles,* "So, too, the reprobate will always be fixed in evil, less from the inability to free themselves from it, than because they wish to be evil" (1.8.4).

2. Jerry Grieser, conversation with the author, 2002.

3. James B. Richards, "Grasping the Truth," *Life at its Best* (blog), accessed September 25, 2015, http://jbrichards.wordpress.com/tag/dr-jim-richards/page/4/.

4. I first heard this proverb from a dear friend and mentor, Dr. Jim Richards; for more information about Jim and his ministry, visit www.impactministries.com.

ABOUT THE AUTHOR

LUCAS MILES is a writer, speaker, life coach, film producer, and pastor. He pours energy and passion into helping others understand how God's grace works on a practical level in all areas of life.

Lucas is the senior pastor of Oasis Granger (www.oasisgranger. com), a church community he and his wife, Krissy, planted in 2004. He is also president of the Oasis Network for Churches (www.oasnet.org), a multifaceted church-planting organization, which services churches in more than ten countries. He frequently appears on television, in churches, on podcasts, at universities, and at conferences throughout the United States and abroad.

In addition to his work in the church, Lucas also maintains a strong presence in the entertainment industry. As the principal and founder of Miles Media, Inc., Lucas is committed to creating films with a purpose. Together, Lucas and Miles Media have a growing catalog of feature films under their belt, including *Rodeo Girl*, *Crowning Jules*, and *The Penitent Thief*, and are currently in development for several TV pilots and additional feature film projects.

Whether in the church, in the entertainment industry, or in the lives of everyday people, Lucas seeks to influence everyone with the truth of the gospel and help remind them that God's goodness knows no bounds. Lucas and Krissy have been married since 2001 and they reside in Granger, Indiana, with their Doberman named Kenya.

IF YOU ENJOYED THIS BOOK, WILL YOU CONSIDER SHARING THE MESSAGE WITH OTHERS?

Mention the book in a blog post or through Facebook, Twitter, Pinterest, or upload a picture through Instagram.

Recommend this book to those in your small group, book club, workplace, and classes.

Head over to facebook.com/worthypublishing, "LIKE" the page, and post a comment as to what you enjoyed the most.

Tweet "I recommend reading #GoodGod by @LucasMiles // @worthypub"

Pick up a copy for someone you know who would be challenged and encouraged by this message.

Write a book review online.

WORTHY®
PUBLISHING

Visit us at worthypublishing.com

twitter.com/worthypub

worthypub.tumblr.com

facebook.com/worthypublishing

pinterest.com/worthypub

instagram.com/worthypub

youtube.com/worthypublishing